NO OTHER GODS

Dr. Phil Fernandes

xulon PRESS

Xulon Press
11350 Random Hills Road
Suite 800
Fairfax, VA 22030
(703) 279-6511
XulonPress.com

To order additional copies, call 1-866-909-BOOK (2665).

DEDICATION

This book is dedicated to the following people:

my wife Cathy
my daughter Melissa and her husband Tim Smith
my grandson Nathan
my parents Joe and Angie Fernandes

CONTENTS

INTRODUCTION

This book deals with apologetics, the defense of the Christian faith. The first three chapters discuss introductory matters. Chapter one shows that apologetics is a biblical practice, while chapter two refutes fideism, the idea that religious beliefs cannot and should not be defended. Chapter three gives the reader an overview of the history of Christian apologetics.

Chapter four begins my case for Christianity. In chapter four, the concept of universal truth and man's ability to know the truth are defended. In chapter five a cumulative case for God is presented. It will be shown that the existence of a personal God is the most plausible explanation for key aspects of human experience.

Chapters six and seven show the Bible to be a historically reliable document, while chapter eight provides evidence for Christ's resurrection from the dead. Chapter nine argues for Christ's deity (i.e., He is God incarnate), whereas chapter ten shows the Bible to be the inspired Word of God.

The appendixes discuss three unique apologists and their methods of defending the faith: Gordon Clark, Cornelius Van Til, and Blaise Pascal. The ancient creed of

1 Corinthinas 15:3-8 will also be examined, showing it to be extremely early evidence for Christ's resurrection from the dead.

It is my prayer that the believing reader will not only gain knowledge from this book, but that he will also grow closer to the Lord Jesus in his walk with Him. If you are a nonbeliever, I beseech you to examine the evidence presented in this book with an open mind, for the God of the Bible is the one true God. There are no other Gods.

CHAPTER 1

THE BIBLICAL BASIS FOR CHRISTIAN APOLOGETICS

A pologetics comes from the Greek word apologia, meaning "a verbal defense, a speech in defense."[1] Therefore, apologetics is that branch of Christian theology that is dedicated to defending the beliefs of biblical Christianity. Though Christian laymen and ministers usually know how to share their faith, they are often unable to defend it. Due to the anti-Christian climate currently prevalent in America, believers need to be informed about this discipline.

Apologetics is a biblical concept. The word apologia is found in Peter's first epistle. Peter declares, "sanctify Christ as Lord in your hearts, always being ready to make a defense to everyone who asks you to give an account for the hope that is in you, yet with gentleness and reverence" (3:15).[2] In this passage, the word apologia is translated "defense."[3]

Apologetics has two functions.[4] Negatively, it refutes belief systems that oppose Christianity, and, positively, it defends the essential truths of the Christian faith.

Apologetics is vital to the Christian church today. Those who share the gospel must also defend the gospel. People are seeking answers to their questions. Through apologetics we can find those answers. We can remove intellectual stumbling blocks that stand between lost souls and Christ. We can communicate the gospel in such a way that the "modern" man will understand it. We must, as the inspired writer instructs us, "contend earnestly for the faith" (Jude 3).

There are three types of apologetic methods.[5] The traditional method assumes neutral ground between Christians and non-Christians, and argues from agreed upon premises to Christian beliefs. The presuppositional method rejects neutral ground between Christians and non-Christians. Rather than arguing to Christianity, the presuppositional approach assumes Christianity to be true and then refutes the non-Christian world view. The verificational method presupposes the truth of Christianity like the presuppositional camp. However, the verificational approach admits enough neutral ground between Christians and non-Christians to allow the Christian world view to be tested and confirmed.

There are at least seven different branches of apologetics.[6] Philosophical apologetics deals with arguments for God's existence, theories of religious language, and the problem of evil. Historical apologetics presents historical evidences for the Christian faith, while scientific apologetics utilizes scientific evidences for the existence of a personal God. Psychological apologetics appeals to the will and emotions of man and argues for the absurdity of life without God and focuses on man's innate thirst for God. Testimonial apologetics uses the evidence of changed lives and divine intervention to defend the Christian faith. Cultural apologetics argues for the truth of the Christian world view by showing the devastating effects on western culture due to the decline in Christian influence on society. Comparative religious apologetics refutes the beliefs of non-Christian systems of thought that contradict Christianity.

In the remainder of this chapter, the biblical basis of apologetics will be examined. Some scholars believe that the gospel should not be defended. These scholars are called fideists.[7] They maintain that one's beliefs should not be rationally defended. Instead, according to this school of thought, one should accept his theological views by a leap of blind faith. One should not look for or provide evidence for religious beliefs. To do so, according to fideists, is to elevate human reason above divine revelation.

If fideism is true, then apologetics is an unbiblical exercise. However, if the practice of apologetics is found to be based in the scriptures, then fideism is an unbiblical system.

THE BIBLE COMMANDS BELIEVERS TO DEFEND THE FAITH

The Bible clearly teaches that Christians are to defend the faith. In fact, believers are commanded to do apologetics. The apostle Peter instructs believers to always be "ready to make a defense" of the Christian hope (1 Peter 3:15).

Jude, the half-brother of Christ, also commands Christians to defend the faith. He tells believers to "contend earnestly for the faith which was once for all delivered to the saints" (Jude 3).

The apostle Paul states that those who are appointed as elders or overseers of local churches should be able to do more than just teach sound biblical doctrine. Paul states that those who hold this office must also be able "to refute those who contradict" the teachings of the Bible (Titus 1:9). In Paul's letter to the Colossian believers, he made the following statement:

> Conduct yourselves with wisdom toward out-
> siders, making the most of the opportunity. Let
> your speech always be with grace, seasoned, as it
> were, with salt, so that you may know how you
> should respond to each person (Colossians 4:5-6).

From these biblical passages, it becomes sufficiently
clear that the Word of God commands believers to defend
the faith. Therefore, the accusations of the fideists are false.
Apologetics is biblical.

THE BIBLE SPEAKS OF NATURAL REVELATION

The Bible not only commands Christians to defend
the faith, but also speaks of God revealing Himself in
nature.[8] This is called natural revelation. Natural revelation
is also known as general revelation since it gives evidence of
God's existence to all mankind.[9] When God made Himself
known to man in the Bible, He miraculously had to guide
human authors to record His Word without error. This is
why the Bible is called supernatural revelation (also known
as special revelation). However, in natural revelation no
supernatural work of God is needed. God has given evidence
of His existence in the universe He created. The Bible
declares the following regarding God's revelation of
Himself in nature:

> The heavens are telling of the glory of God; and
> their expanse is declaring the work of His hands.
> Day to day pours forth speech, and night to night
> reveals knowledge (Psalm 19:1-2).

> For the wrath of God is revealed from heaven
> against all ungodliness and unrighteousness of

men, who suppress the truth in unrighteousness, because that which is known about God is evident within them; for God made it evident to them. For since the creation of the world His invisible attributes, His eternal power and divine nature, have been clearly seen, being understood through what has been made, so that they are without excuse. For even though they knew God, they did not honor Him as God, or give thanks; but they became futile in their speculations, and their foolish heart was darkened. Professing to be wise, they became fools . . . (Romans 1:18-22).

These passages teach that though no one has ever seen the invisible God, the visible work of His hands can be seen in His creation. If someone finds a watch, he knows a watchmaker must exist, though he has never seen him.[10] Therefore, when man sees the beauty and order of the universe, he knows that it must have been caused by an intelligent and powerful Being.

Since God has revealed Himself in nature, Christians can argue from the effect (the universe) to its cause (God). To gaze at the starry sky on a clear night and still believe that the universe is a product of chance is an insult to human reason.

Another aspect of natural revelation deals with the fact that God has revealed His law in the conscience of each person. The apostle Paul affirms this in the following words:

For when Gentiles who do not have the Law do instinctively the things of the Law, these, not having the Law, are a law to themselves, in that they show the work of the Law written in their hearts, their conscience bearing witness, and their thoughts alternately accusing or else defending them . . . (Romans 2:14-15).

Because God has given all men a glimpse of His moral law in their consciences, believers can argue from this moral law to the existence of the moral Lawgiver. Since the moral laws are above all men, the moral Lawgiver must also be above all men. Since evidence for God can be found in nature, philosophical apologetics (which argues for God's existence from the evidence of nature) is a biblical practice.

THE BIBLE SPEAKS OF HISTORICAL EVIDENCES

As mentioned above, the Bible teaches that God has revealed Himself to man in nature. However, besides this evidence in nature, the Bible declares that evidence for the Christian faith can also be found in history.[11] While attempting to prove the resurrection of Christ from the dead, as well as the future resurrection of all believers, the apostle Paul lists the eyewitnesses of Christ's post-resurrection appearances:

> For I deliver to you as of first importance what I also received, that Christ died for our sins according to the Scriptures, and that He was buried, and that He was raised on the third day according to the Scriptures, and that He appeared to Cephas, then to the twelve. After that He appeared to more than five hundred brethren at one time, most of whom remain until now, but some have fallen asleep; then He appeared to James, then to all the apostles; and last of all, as it were to one untimely born, He appeared to me also (1 Corinthians 15:3-8).

From this passage it is clear that the apostle Paul was willing to refer to the evidence of eyewitness testimony in order to provide a defense for the truth of the gospel. Therefore, there is a biblical basis for historical apologetics. Historical apologetics utilizes historical evidences to argue for the truth of the Christian faith.

THE EARLY CHURCH DEFENDED THE FAITH

The Bible commands believers to do apologetics. The scriptures speak of both natural revelation and historical evidences. And, finally, the early church did apologetics. The apostles defended the gospel.

The apostle Peter defended the faith. On the day of Pentecost, Peter preached his famous sermon. Three thousand people were saved and added to the church. During that sermon Peter stated, "This Jesus God raised up again, to which we are all witnesses" (Acts 2:32). Peter often defended the faith during his sermons by appealing to eyewitness testimony (Acts 3:15; 5:30-32; 10:39-41).

The apostle John also defended the faith. In fact, he claimed that the main purpose for writing his Gospel was to provide eyewitness accounts of Christ's miraculous life in order to persuade others to believe (John 20:30-31).

Luke willingly shared proof of Christ's claims. When Luke wrote the book of Acts, he stated that Christ "presented Himself alive, after His suffering, by many convincing proofs, appearing to them over a period of forty days" (Acts 1:1-3). Luke shared with Theophilus, the person to whom the book of Acts was addressed, eyewitness evidence of the post-resurrection appearances of Christ. Thus, Theophilus would not have to exercise blind faith in order to believe. Luke knew that biblical faith is based upon evidence, not an irrational leap.

The apostle Paul was also a defender of the faith. The scriptures say that he kept "confounding the Jews who lived at Damascus by proving that this Jesus is the Christ" (Acts 9:22). Paul's custom was to enter various synagogues and reason with the Jews from the scriptures (Acts 17:1-3; 18:4). If the Jews rejected the gospel message, he would then go and proclaim it to the Gentiles:

> And he entered the synagogue and continued speaking out boldly for three months, reasoning and persuading them about the kingdom of God. But when some were becoming hardened and disobedient, speaking evil of the Way before the multitude, he withdrew from them and took away the disciples, reasoning daily in the school of Tyrannus. And this took place for two years, so that all who lived in Asia heard the word of the Lord, both Jews and Greeks (Acts 19:8-10).

While in Athens, Paul stood on Mars Hill and preached one of his greatest sermons (Acts 17:16-34). There, he was confronted by Greek philosophers: the Epicureans and the Stoics. The Epicurean philosophers believed that God did not exist, while the Stoic philosophers equated God with the universe.

Paul noticed that the Athenians had devoted a statue to "an Unknown God." Paul then claimed to personally know this God of whom they were ignorant. Twice he quoted from the works of ancient Greek poets to establish his case as he began to share the gospel. Finally, when Paul spoke of God raising Jesus from the dead, many of the Greek philosophers sneered, while others asked Paul if he would be willing to speak to them again. Though the idea of a bodily resurrection had been repugnant to the Greeks since the days of Plato (427-347BC),[12] some Greeks were willing to give Paul a second hearing. This was probably due to the fact that he had proved himself to be well-read in Greek philosophy, even though he held the belief of Christ's bodily resurrection.

As demonstrated in Paul's case, apologetics enables a person to speak to the "intellectual elite." Paul chose to "become all things to all men" (1 Corinthians 9:19-22). He was willing to use anti-Christian philosophies in order to refute the false beliefs of his listeners and to lead them to Christ. No defender of the faith can do less.

And, finally, Apollos used apologetics. He was a great defender of the faith. Luke records this about him:

> Now a certain Jew named Apollos, an Alexandrian by birth, an eloquent man, came to Ephesus; and he was mighty in the scriptures . . . for he powerfully refuted the Jews in public, demonstrating by the scriptures that Jesus was the Christ" (Acts 18:24-28).

CONCLUSION

Apologetics is taught in the Bible. The Bible commands us to defend the faith. The scriptures also speak of natural revelation and historical evidences for the Christian faith. And finally, the early church defended the faith. Apologetics is squarely based in the Bible.

ENDNOTES

[1] W. E. Vine, *Expository Dictionary of New Testament Words* (Grand Rapids: Zondervan Publishing House, 1952), 61.

[2] *New American Standard Bible* (La Habra: The Lockman Foundation, 1973). All biblical quotations are taken from the NASB unless otherwise noted.

[3] *The Zondervan Parallel New Testament In Greek and English* (Grand Rapids: Zondervan Bible Publishers, 1975), 691.

[4] Earle E. Cairns, *Christianity Through the Centuries* (Grand Rapids: Zondervan Publishing House, 1981), 105.

[5] Scott R. Burson and Jerry L. Walls, C. S. Lewis & Francis Schaeffer (Downers Grove: InterVarsity Press, 1998), 20.

[6]Phil Fernandes, *A Survey of Christian Apologetics: Examining Christian Apologetics in All its Branches* (unpublished Ph.D. dissertation: Greenwich University, 1996), 91-97.

[7]Norman L. Geisler, *Christian Apologetics* (Grand Rapids: Baker Book House, 1976), 58-59.

[8]Henry Clarence Thiessen, *Lectures in Systematic Theology* (Grand Rapids: Eerdmans Publishing, 1979), 7-8.

[9]Ibid.

[10]John Hick, ed. *The Existence of God* (New York: The Macmillan Company, 1964), 99-103.

[11]Ibid., 8-9.

[12]William S. Sahakian, *History of Philosophy* (New York: Harper Perennial, 1968), 55-56.

CHAPTER 2

FIDEISM: THE ENEMY OF APOLOGETICS

Fideism is the belief that religious faith cannot be defended through the use of philosophical, historical, or scientific evidences. Religious faith is viewed as a leap of faith into the nonrational realm. One makes an ultimate commitment apart from any evidence. Objective truths are not considered as important as a person's subjective beliefs, for religious truth is viewed as personal, not propositional.[1]

Obviously, fideism is the antithesis of apologetics. Apologetics is the defense of the Christian faith; fideism claims that the Christian faith cannot be defended. It can only be believed. For this reason, fideism is the enemy of apologetics. They cannot both be true. In this chapter, the views of several men whose ideas are associated with fideism will be discussed. This chapter will close with a critique of the fideist position.

TERTULLIAN

Though Tertullian, a second century Christian

21

thinker, was a great defender of the faith, he has often been mistaken for a fideist. Tertullian stated, "I believe because it is absurd."[2] However, Norman Geisler and Paul Feinberg point out that Tertullian was not saying that he held to the idea that contradictions are true. Rather, he merely meant that he accepted the gospel as true even though the world considered it foolishness.[3] In other words, Tertullian was merely echoing the teachings of the apostle Paul (1 Corinthians 1:18-31).

Tertullian also stated, "What indeed has Athens to do with Jerusalem?"[4] Obviously, he was contrasting Greek philosophy and Christian theology. Still, he was probably not opposed to all philosophy, since he often used reason to defend the faith. Tertullian was simply opposed to all anti-Christian philosophy. He refused to judge the gospel by human reason. Rather, he judged the reason of men by God's revelation in the Bible. Still, this did not make him a fideist. He believed that the truth of Christianity had been proven by the blood shed by Christian martyrs.5 In other words, he accepted the evidence of eyewitness testimonies as establishing the truth of the Christian revelation. That being proven, he then judged the philosophies of men by God's wisdom.

Hence, Tertullian was not a fideist. Still, he is often quoted out of context to promote fideism. For that reason, he has been discussed here.

BLAISE PASCAL

Blaise Pascal (1623-1662) was not a complete fideist. He argued for the truth of the Christian faith, something a fideist would not do. However, it is the way that Pascal defended the faith that moved him closer to fideism. This was due to the fact that he criticized rationalism to the point that he questioned the reliability of man's reasoning processes. In Pascal's thinking, man must submit his reason to his will.[6] The mind must bow to the heart.

Pascal did not consider Christianity to be against reason. He merely emphasized the point that God cannot be found through human reason alone.[7] It was here that Pascal developed his famous "wager argument" for God's existence. Pascal considered the rational evidence for or against God's existence to be even. Reason cannot decide. One must choose with one's will whether or not to believe that God exists since the odds are even. The mind must give way to the will. Each person must decide to choose or not to choose God. Pascal pleads with his readers to choose God. If his readers choose God and He does not really exist, they will have lost nothing. But, if his readers choose God and He does exist, they gain eternal life. On the other hand, if his readers wager against God and win, they win nothing, but if they lose, they lose everything.[8]

Though many have found this argument convincing, it has opened the door to fideism. For Pascal declared that man must test truth with his heart, not with his mind.[9] Future professing Christian thinkers went far beyond Pascal's views. Subjective beliefs were beginning to surpass objective truth in importance in the history of philosophical thought.

GOTTHOLD EPHRAIM LESSING

Gotthold Ephraim Lessing (1729-1781) was a critic of the Bible who denied biblical inerrancy. He taught that religious beliefs could not be proven through reason or historical evidences.[10] He was a fideist in the truest sense. He held that faith rested on subjective experience rather than on objective evidence. He believed that religions should be judged by their effect on the moral conduct of its followers.[11] Evidence for or against religious truth claims were irrelevant.

Lessing imagined an "ugly ditch" between faith and historical facts.[12] This ditch could not be crossed. No one can know for sure if the Jesus of the gospels is in fact the true Jesus of history. Religious beliefs could not be defended by appealing to objective facts. Only practical results could be used to determine the worth of a religious system. Testing religious truths is a subjective, inward task. Any appeal to objective evidence is futile.

SOREN KIERKEGAARD

Soren Kierkegaard (1813-1855), the famous Danish philosopher, is known as the "father of modern existentialism." Kierkegaard believed that there were three stages of life: the aesthetic, the ethical, and the religious.[13] Each stage is separated by a feeling of despair. Also, each stage can only be crossed by a leap of faith.[14]

A person lives in the aesthetic stage when he exists for his own pleasure. In this stage, the person is self-centered. Through a leap of faith, a person can enter into the ethical stage. Here, duty comes first. This person is law-centered. But when the overwhelming feeling of despair and futility comes, the person can, through another leap of faith, arrive at the religious stage. In this stage, the person is God-centered.[15]

Kierkegaard believed religious truth is personal and subjective, not propositional and objective. He felt that subjective truth is of greater importance than objective truth. To leap into the religious stage, one must leave the realm of reason. Kierkegaard is not saying that religious faith is irrational. He merely means that it is nonrational. Reason does not apply. It is an act of the will that is necessary. A leap of blind faith (apart from reason) is needed to accept religious truth.

For Kierkegaard, God's existence cannot be proven.[16] Religious faith comes from the heart, not the mind. An act of the will is needed, not an act of the intellect. Since religious truth is subjective and personal, there is no test for truth which can be applied.[17]

KARL BARTH

Karl Barth (1886-1968) rebelled against liberal theology and started neo-orthodoxy. He rejected the liberal view that man was basically good.[18] Barth, though accepting a critical view of the Bible, recognized that man is limited and sinful. He taught that God is "wholly other" than man. He considered the Bible a human book which contains errors. However, it becomes revelation from God to the individual in the moment of crisis. This crisis is the crisis of faith. It is that moment when a person recognizes God's condemnation of all human effort and that deliverance comes only through God. At this moment, the Holy Spirit uses the Bible as His instrument to bring about a personal encounter between the individual and God. During this encounter, no communication of information takes place. In Barth's eyes, revelation is personal encounter with God, not the making known of information.[19]

Barth taught that sin blinds man from finding the truth. Only the Holy Spirit can open man's spiritual eyes so that he can see God. The divine-human encounter is purely a subjective experience.[20]

In this encounter, man encounters God. However, man does not encounter any objective truths about Him.[21]

In Barth's thought, man is incapable of receiving any revelation from God through nature.[22] Man's spiritual blindness can only be removed by a contact sovereignly initiated by the Holy Spirit.[23] Obviously, Barth is opposed to apologetics. There is no need to defend the divine-human encounter since it cannot even be expressed. There is also no need to defend the Bible since it is a human book with errors. Therefore, for Barth and all other fideists, Christianity is to be accepted by faith. It should not be defended.

CONCLUSION

In chapter one of this work, apologetics was shown

to be biblically based. First, it was concluded that the Bible commands believers to do apologetics (1 Peter 3:15; Colossians 4:5-6; Titus 1:7-9; Jude 3). Second, the scriptures speak of God revealing Himself in nature (Psalm 19:1; 94:9; Romans 1:18-22; 2:14-15). Third, God's Word speaks of historical evidences for the Christian faith (1 Corinthians 15:3-8). And, fourth, the early church defended the faith. Examples were given: Peter, John, Luke, Paul, and Apollos. In short, by showing that apologetics is biblically based, fideism has been proven unscriptural.

Still, there is a lesson one can learn from fideists. Though Thomas Aquinas was one of the greatest defenders of the faith, his thought was often misinterpreted as equating faith with intellectual assent to doctrines that could not be proven by reason.[24] This misinterpretation of Aquinas placed faith into the head with reason, rather than in the heart. The biblical concept of faith as a personal trust in Christ for salvation was lost. In reality, Aquinas taught that there was a clear distinction between "faith that" (intellectual assent) and "faith in" (personal trust in Christ). Still, even though misunderstanding of Aquinas' thought prevailed, the fideists must be credited for reemphasizing the aspect of personal commitment and trust. However, in the process, they have de-emphasized reason. Though a personal relationship with Jesus must be stressed, before one can believe in the Jesus of the Bible, one must believe the facts about Him. Revelation without content is no revelation at all.

If one's apologetics is to be biblical, one must learn this lesson from the fideists. The defense of the faith can lead a person to give intellectual assent to the facts of the gospel. Still, the person must choose, by an act of his or her will, to personally appropriate the truths of the gospel. Mere head knowledge will save no one. A decision of the heart is needed. Though belief in the claims of Christ is necessary for salvation, one must still personally trust in Christ to be saved. One must never turn the gospel into a mere creed by removing the personal, experiential aspects of Christianity. Even so, the fideist has faltered on the other extreme by removing the intellectual content from the gospel. When this has been done, there is no gospel left at all. Gospel means good news. There can be no gospel if there is no news.

The Christian faith contains both objective and subjective elements. Effective defenders of the faith will proclaim both. To neglect one at the expense of the other is to move away from historical Christianity.

ENDNOTES

[1] Geisler, *Apologetics*, 58-59.

[2] Ibid., 47.

[3] Norman L. Geisler and Paul D. Feinberg, *Introduction to Philosophy*, (Grand Rapids: Baker Book House, 1980), 262.

[4] Geisler, *Apologetics*, 47.

[5] Tim Dowley, ed., *The History of Christianity* (Oxford: Lion Publishing, 1977), 112.

[6] Geisler, *Apologetics*, 48.

[7] Ibid.

[8] Ibid., 49.

[9] Ibid., 50.

[10] Frederick Copleston, *A History of Philosophy* (New York: Doubleday, 1960), book 2, vol. 6, 126-131.

[11] Ibid.

[12] Millard J. Erickson, *The Word Became Flesh* (Grand Rapids: Baker Book House, 1991), 115.

[13] Sahakian, 343.

[14] Geisler, *Apologetics*, 50.

[15] Ibid.

[16] Ibid., 52-53.

[17] Ibid., 53.

[18] Cairns, 445.

[19] Ibid.

[20] Ibid.

[21] Geisler, *Apologetics,* 53-56.

[22] Ibid, 55.

[23] Ibid.

[24] William Lane Craig, *Apologetics, An Introduction* (Chicago: Moody Press, 1984), 9-10.

CHAPTER 3

A HISTORY OF APOLOGETICS:

ITS DEFENDERS AND ANTAGONISTS

=====================

Christian apologetics is not new. In chapter one it was shown that the apostles themselves utilized apologetics on numerous occasions. In this chapter, it will be demonstrated that apologetics has continued throughout church history. Before discussing the history of Christian apologetics, three points need to be stressed.

First, some of the apologists (those who defend the faith against external opposition) that will be discussed in this chapter were not orthodox in all areas of their theology. Still, they professed faith in Christ and defended some orthodox aspect of the faith. Therefore, they deserve mention here.

Second, some of these defenders of the faith could be classified as apologists, while others did polemical work—they refuted heresies that developed within the professing church rather than from external opposition. Since some of the heresies refuted by the polemical scholars were later revived as apologetic issues, both types of defending the faith will be discussed in this chapter.

Third, several non-Christian thinkers greatly influenced the history of Christian apologetics. Therefore, mention will be made concerning their views despite the fact that they did not profess faith in Christ. Keeping these three points in mind, a brief overview of the history of the defense of the Christian faith will be given. This will establish the fact that apologetics (as well as polemics) has always been practiced by the church.

THE FIRST CENTURY

As was mentioned in chapter one, the apostolic church defended the faith. Peter often used eyewitness evidence to defend the resurrection of Christ from the dead. John used his own eyewitness accounts of Christ's miracles to persuade others to believe. Luke referred to the post-resurrection appearances of Jesus to establish his case. Paul reasoned with both Jews and Greeks in his attempts to lead them to Christ. And, Apollos debated Jews and proved that Jesus was the Christ (the one anointed by God to redeem Israel).

THE SECOND CENTURY

Ignatius, the Bishop of Antioch, was martyred early in the second century (between 110 and 115AD).[1] During this time he wrote seven letters. In his letters to Smyrna and Talles, he condemned a gnostic heresy called Docetism.[2] Gnosticism made salvation dependent on secret knowledge.[3] The Gnostics believed that all matter was evil while spirit was good.[4] Docetism was the gnostic view that since matter is evil, Jesus only appeared to have a body; He was actually only a spirit being without a real body. Docetists believed that only a phantom died on the cross. Ignatius refuted this view by declaring Jesus to be "truly" of human flesh and stating that He was "truly" put to death in the flesh for our sins.[5]

Justin Martyr (100-165) was converted to Christianity from paganism. In his writing entitled Dialogue With Trypho, he answered Trypho's accusations that Christians violate the Mosaic Law since they worship a human being.[6] Justin Martyr argued from Old Testament passages that Jesus is God and that He fulfilled the Mosaic Law.

Aristides, Tatian, Athenagoras, and Theophilus all argued that Christianity is superior to the pagan religions.[7] The Epistle to Diognetus and The Epistle of Barnabas, both by unknown authors, presented rational defenses of the Christian faith and presented Christ's death as adequate for salvation.[8]

Irenaeus became the Bishop of Lyons in 177AD.[9] He wrote a work entitled Against Heresies. In this work, he refuted Gnosticism by teaching that 1) evil is not co-eternal with God, 2) matter is not evil, and 3) Jesus rose bodily from the dead.[10] Irenaeus also wrote Proof of the Apostolic Preaching. In this writing, he demonstrated that Jesus fulfilled Old Testament prophecies.[11]

THE THIRD CENTURY

Tertullian wrote between 196 and 212AD. In Apology, he defended Christian beliefs against heresy and argued that Christians should be tolerated, not persecuted.[12] Tertullian also wrote five books called Against Marcion. In these works, he defended the use of the Old Testament by Christians and the oneness of God.[13] In another work, Against Praxeas, Tertullian defended the doctrine of the Trinity (God eternally exists as three equal Persons).[14]

Origen (185-254) wrote Against Celsus, in which he

answered pagan objections to the Christian faith.[15] Unfortunately, Origen himself taught the heretical doctrines of the preexistence of souls and universal salvation, and was later condemned by the church.[16]

THE FOURTH CENTURY

Athanasius (300-373) refuted Arius, a heretic who taught that Jesus was a created being and a lesser god than the Father.[17] Athanasius rightly taught that Jesus is equal with the Father and existed from all eternity with Him. The church ruled in favor of the Athanasian view and condemned the Arian heresy.[18] This was eventually made clear in the Nicene Creed.

Ambrose (339-397) helped to complete the overthrow of Arianism in the Western Church.[19] Unfortunately, it has been revived in modern times by the Jehovah's Witnesses.

Basil the Great (330-379) also opposed Arianism. He defended the Trinity by affirming the Deity of the Holy Spirit. He helped to define the Trinity as one in substance but three in persons.[20]

THE FIFTH CENTURY

Augustine (354-430) was the Bishop of Hippo in North Africa. As one of the greatest theologians in the history of the church, Augustine wrote many works defending Christianity. Many people consider him to be the greatest church leader in history between the apostle Paul and Martin Luther.

Early in his life, Augustine had accepted a dualistic religion called Manicheanism.[21] This religion taught that God (light) and matter (darkness) are both eternal.[22] The Manicheans believed that both good and evil existed throughout all eternity. This, they reasoned, removed any responsibility from God for the evil that exists in the universe.

Under the preaching of Ambrose, Augustine became a Christian.[23] He began to see that evil was not coeternal with God. Rather, God alone is eternal, and all that He created is good. Yet, by giving angels and men free will, God permitted evil to come into existence. Therefore, evil is a privation (a lack of the good that should be there). Evil does not exist on its own, but must exist in something good (just as rust cannot come into existence without the metal it corrupts). Therefore, Augustine concluded that evil exists as a corruption or perversion of God's perfect creation.[24] God created the universe perfect, but angels and men brought evil into the universe through their free choices. God allows evil and human suffering for the purpose of a greater good.

Augustine was influenced by Plato's doctrine of the invisible world of unchanging, eternal ideas or truths. However, Augustine, unlike Plato, placed these eternal ideas in the mind of God, and argued that we cannot perceive these unchanging truths unless our limited minds are illuminated by God.[25] Augustine reasoned that our minds have knowledge of these eternal, unchanging ideas. But, our minds, since they are limited and changing, cannot be the adequate cause for these eternal, unchanging ideas. Therefore, argued Augustine, only an unchanging, eternal Mind (i.e., God) is the adequate cause of these unchanging, eternal ideas.[26]

Augustine correctly saw and defended the fact that mankind has inherited a corrupted nature from Adam.[27] Augustine's most famous debate was with a monk named Pelagius. Pelagius believed that each person is born in the same state in which Adam was created. Thus, each person is not contaminated by Adam's sin. In Pelagius' view, Adam merely set a bad example for his offspring. It is possible for man to live without sin. Augustine refuted Pelagius by pointing out that the scriptures teach that each person inherits Adam's sin nature. Therefore, no one can please God through human effort. Man must rely on God's grace to be saved.

Though Augustine rightly defended both divine sovereignty and human free will, his later writings exhibited an extreme view of predestination that canceled out any real human freedom in the area of salvation.[28] Man, in Augustine's view, believes in Christ only because God predestined him to do so.

Augustine refuted the skeptics, those who taught that man should suspend judgment on all things. He argued that skepticism is rationally inconsistent since the skeptic claims to suspend judgment on all things, but does not suspend judgment on his skepticism. Augustine also charged that skeptics cannot live consistently with their skepticism, for the skeptic does not suspend judgment when it comes to eating, protecting oneself, etc. Since skepticism fails, knowledge is possible.[29]

Augustine speculated that there was no time before creation; he believed that God created time when He created the universe. Therefore, God exists outside time in eternity. Time is the realm of past, present, and future. Eternity is the realm of the eternal, unchanging now.[30]

In his writings Augustine defended the doctrine of the Trinity, the deity of Christ, and salvation by God's grace. Augustine's two greatest works were Confessions and The City of God. Confessions is an autobiographical work detailing Augustine's conversion. The City of God was Augustine's view of history. It represented his greatest philosophical and apologetic work. For Augustine, the city of God consists of all angels and men who love and serve God, while the city of the Devil is comprised of those angels and men who oppose the God of the Bible. The battle between these two cities manifests itself throughout human history.

THE SIXTH CENTURY

Boethuis (480-524) was educated in both the philosophies of Plato and Aristotle. He wrote five books in defense of Christianity. Boethuis, long before Thomas Aquinas did, applied Aristotle's logic to Christian theology.[31]

THE EIGHTH CENTURY

Alcuin (735-804) was an Anglo-Saxon scholar who led the battle against Adoptionism in Spain.[32] Adoptionism is the heresy that teaches that Jesus was only a man whom God adopted as His son.

At His baptism, Christ was given special powers by God. After God raised Jesus from the dead as a reward for His good works, God adopted Jesus into the Godhead.[33] Alcuin refuted this view by proclaiming the biblical teaching that Jesus is fully God and fully man. Jesus always existed as God, but also took a human nature upon Himself at a point in time.

THE ELEVENTH CENTURY

Anselm (1033-1109) was the archbishop of Canterbury. He was an early scholastic theologian. Scholasticism dates from the eleventh century to the end of the fourteenth century. Scholasticism was an attempt by medieval Christian scholars to use reason to reconcile orthodox Christianity and the philosophy of Aristotle.

Anselm is famous for his ontological argument for God's existence.[34] Anselm believed that God's existence could be proven by reason alone. He concluded that God must exist since His nonexistence is inconceivable. For God is, by definition, the greatest conceivable being. The greatest conceivable being must exist. If He did not exist, then one could conceive of a being greater than Him—a being with the same attributes who did exist. But then this being would be God. Hence, according to Anselm's reasoning, God must exist.[35]

Anselm had another way of stating his ontological argument. He declared that since God is by definition the most perfect being, He must lack no perfection. Since Anselm believed that existence was a perfection, he reasoned that it is impossible for God to lack existence.

Therefore, God must exist.[36] Many philosophers today reject the ontological argument for God's existence. Still, it has provoked much thought and debate even in this modern era.

It should also be noted that Anselm did not limit his apologetics to the ontological argument for God's existence. Anselm also used the cosmological argument when attempting to prove God's existence. He argued from the existence of good things in the world to the existence of the supreme Good.

Anselm also argued for the logical consistency of the incarnation.[37] He reasoned that mankind fell through a man (Adam); therefore, mankind must be redeemed through a man (Christ). By sinning against God, man has robbed God of His glory. Sin is rebellion against God, the ultimately worthy Being. Since God is just, He cannot forgive our sin unless the ultimately worthy sacrifice is provided. The ultimate price must be paid to God's justice. Only God is capable of being the ultimately worthy sacrifice, but He must become a man in order to die. Hence, only the God-man can redeem man. For only God can satisfy the infinite debt that sin has caused. Only an infinite Person can satisfy God's infinite holiness and justice. However, only a man can redeem man, for only a man can die. Therefore, God the Son had to become a man to provide salvation for men. Anselm concluded that there was no other way that man could be saved.

THE TWELFTH CENTURY

Peter Aberlard (1079-1142) was a Catholic monk.

He was a brilliant lecturer and debater.[38] He attempted to reconcile faith and reason. It was his conviction that true Christianity was reasonable and consistent.[39]

THE THIRTEENTH CENTURY

Albert the Great (1206-1280) was a Catholic theologian who utilized the philosophy of Aristotle in his system of thought. His most famous student was Thomas Aquinas. Albert saw a distinction between theology (the study of that which God has supernaturally revealed) and philosophy (the use of human reason to find truth). Still, he recognized the need for both disciplines.[40] One of Albert's greatest contributions to apologetics was his promotion of the study and use of philosophy in Christian thought.[41]

Albert argued for God's existence from the motion in the universe. He, like Aristotle, concluded that there must be an unmoved Mover as the cause of all motion in the universe.[42] Albert was well read in Greek, Jewish, and Arabian philosophy.[43] Still, he remained true to orthodox Christianity and held many beliefs in common with Augustine (though Augustine utilized the philosophy of Plato rather than that of Aristotle).

Albert's thought was never formulated into a completed system. What he began was completed by his great student Thomas Aquinas.[44] Aquinas took Aristotle's philosophical thought and produced a complete synthesis with Christian theology.

Thomas Aquinas (1225-1274) was the greatest scholastic thinker of the middle ages.[45] He was born in Aquino, Italy. As mentioned above, he studied under Albert the Great in Paris and Cologne. Aquinas, like Albert, utilized Aristotle's philosophy in structuring his theological thought, but, unlike Albert, Aquinas developed a complete system.

Aquinas rejected the ontological argument for God's existence. He believed that all human knowledge begins in the senses and that the human mind begins life as a "blank slate" upon which nothing is written. Aquinas called this aspect of the human mind the "receptive mind."[46] He taught that everything in the mind was first in the senses except the mind itself.[47] In other words, we start life with no data in our minds, though our minds have the innate ability to draw information from sense experience.[48] The mind has the capacity to draw more out of sense data than sense data itself. The mind does this by reasoning and making judgments on the information gained through sense experiences. Aquinas referred to this aspect of the mind as the "active mind."[49] Still, knowledge must begin with sense experience. Therefore, one cannot argue from the idea of God to His existence (the ontological argument).[50] Instead, one must argue from the elements of the physical world to its ultimate Cause.[51] This is why Aquinas used the cosmological and teleological arguments for God's existence. The cosmological argument reasons that finite things such as the universe need an infinite Cause. The teleological argument concludes that the design and order in the universe is evidence for the existence of an intelligent Designer of the universe.

Aquinas is famous for his five ways to prove God's existence.[52] The first four ways are cosmological arguments, while the fifth way is a teleological argument.[53] In his first way to prove God's existence, Aquinas argued from the movement or change in the universe to an unmoved Mover. Second, Aquinas argued from effects in the universe (which cannot account for their own present existence) to their uncaused Cause. Third, Aquinas argued that the existence of beings that have the possibility of nonexistence must have their existence grounded by a Being which has no possibility of nonexistence. Fourth, Aquinas reasoned that since there are different degrees of perfections among beings, there must be a most perfect Being. And, in Aquinas' fifth way he concluded that since non-intelligent nature progresses towards a definite goal, it must be directed towards this goal by an intelligent Being.[54]

Aquinas accepted the Genesis account of creation; therefore, he believed that the universe had a beginning. However, following Aristotle's reasoning, he did not believe that man could rationally prove that the universe had a beginning. According to Aquinas, the beginning of the universe was something that had to be accepted by faith in Scripture.[55]

Aquinas also attempted to solve the problem of evil.[56] He agreed with Augustine that God did not create evil, but that evil is merely a corruption of God's good creation. God did however, according to Aquinas, create the possibility for evil by giving man and angels free will. Fallen men and angels brought evil into the universe by choosing to rebel against God. Aquinas reasoned that God allows evil for the purpose of a greater good. The possibility of evil is necessary in order for man to have free will. Since God is all-good and all-powerful, He will one day defeat evil. He accomplishes this through the atoning work of Christ.

Aquinas agreed with Aristotle concerning the first principles of knowledge. These principles cannot be proven by reason; they are self-evident. We must utilize them when we reason; we cannot think or communicate without them. These principles are: identity (being is being), noncontradiction (being is not nonbeing), excluded middle (either being or nonbeing), causality (nonbeing cannot cause being), and finality (every being acts for an end).[57]

Aquinas drew a distinction between essence (what something is) and existence (that something is). Only in God essence and existence are identical. Aquinas also drew a distinction between act and potency. Some beings could possibly exist but do not. Other beings actually exist but have the potential for nonexistence (all created beings).

Only God is pure act; He actually exists and has no potential for nonexistence.[58]

Aquinas solved the problem of religious language. Aquinas rejected univocal knowledge of God. Words used of the infinite God cannot mean exactly the same when used and applied to finite man. For God's existence far transcends man's existence. On the other hand, if words used of man have totally different meanings when applied to God, then man can have no knowledge of God whatsoever. This rules out equivocal knowledge of God. Aquinas settled this dilemma by his doctrine of analogical language. A term used both of God and man will be defined the same. Still, the term will not be attributed to man and God in exactly the same way. The terms will be infinitely applied to God, but finitely applied to man. Man can be finitely good, but only God is infinitely good. We must remove all limitations from terms before attributing them to God.[59]

Aquinas believed that God has revealed Himself in both nature and the scriptures. Some truths can be proven by reason, but others (like the doctrine of the Trinity) are above reason and must be accepted by faith alone.[60] Still, there is much evidence for accepting the Bible as God's Word. In fact, miracles and philosophical arguments confirm the truth of Christianity.[61]

Aquinas spent much time philosophically defending the orthodox attributes of God. In Aquinas' thought, God is immutable, eternal, simple (not composed of parts), one, and infinite.[62] Since God is the cause of all perfections that exist, He must have all these perfections. Since He is an infinite Being, He must have all these perfections to an infinite degree.

Aquinas differentiated between "belief that" (which deals with the intellect of man) and "belief in" (which deals with the will of man). A person who believes that God exists may still refuse to believe in Him for salvation.[63]

Thomas Aquinas was one of the greatest defenders of the Christian faith of all time. To this day, many scholars rely heavily upon his thought. Whether Catholic or Protestant, scholars who utilize his system of apologetics are called Thomists.

Bonaventure (1221-1274) was a contemporary of Thomas Aquinas. Bonaventure used many different arguments for God's existence. He reasoned that our idea of imperfections assumes the existence of the Perfect (by which the imperfections are compared). Bonaventure argued that since beings that are produced exist, there must exist a first Cause of their existence. The existence of changeable beings declares the existence of an unchangeable Being. Bonaventure stated that since from nothing, nothing can come, there must be a self-existent Being as the ground of all other existence. Beings which have the possibility of nonexistence necessitate the existence of a Being which cannot not exist.[64]

Bonaventure believed that God's existence is self-evident to all men. God's existence is a truth that is naturally implanted in the human mind. Still, he viewed this knowledge to be dim and implicit, rather than obvious and explicit. He considered the atheist to be one who has chosen not to reflect upon this truth. Thus, God's existence can be doubted by men.[65]

Bonaventure also utilized Anselm's ontological argument for God's existence. Since God is the greatest conceivable being, He must exist. For if He did not, one could conceive of a being greater than Him, a being that did exist. Therefore, God must exist.[66]

Bonaventure borrowed from Augustine as well. He reasoned from the existence of eternal truths to the existence of an eternal Mind.[67]

Bonaventure, however, had a major disagreement with Thomas Aquinas. Aquinas believed that it was philosophically possible for the universe to be eternal, while Bonaventure believed it could be philosophically proven that the universe had a beginning. Both men agreed that the universe was created and was not eternal. This was clear from the scriptures. However, Aquinas agreed with Aristotle that there is nothing logically contradictory with an eternal universe. To refute this view, Bonaventure showed that it is impossible to both add to an infinite number and to pass through an infinite series. For if the universe is eternal, then present events would be adding to the infinite number of past events. But the infinite cannot be added to since it is already infinite. Also, if the universe is eternal, then one could never reach the present moment since one would have to pass through an infinite series of past events to arrive at the present. This is impossible due to the fact that no matter how many past events are crossed, there will always be an infinite number more to pass through before the present moment can be reached. Therefore, Bonaventure showed in convincing fashion that it is philosophically contradictory to hold to the possibility of an eternal universe.[68]

John Duns Scotus (1265-1308) argued that if any being cannot cause its own continued existence, then it cannot ground the existence of another being. Therefore, there must exist a totally independent Being who is the ground of all dependent existence.[69]

Scotus, like Aquinas before him, was not arguing for the cause of the beginning of the existence of dependent beings. Rather, he argued for the cause of the continuing existence of dependent beings.

THE FOURTEENTH CENTURY

William of Ockham (1290-1384) was a Franciscan monk. He denied rational proofs for God's existence. He taught that God was known by faith alone. Man could not reason to God.[70] This led to a decline in philosophical apologetics that culminated in the thought of Kant, Hegel, and Kierkegaard. Kant denied that man could know reality as it exists in itself. Man could only know reality as it appeared to him.[71] Hegel taught that all contradictory views would be reconciled, thus denying that truth is absolute.[72] Kierkegaard declared that religious beliefs were nonrational and must be accepted through a leap of blind faith.[73] Since Kant, Hegel, and Kierkegaard have greatly influenced contemporary thought, William of Ockham's impact on current religious and secular dialogue should not be underestimated. Ockham is also famous for his principle, called "Ockham's razor," which declares the simplest explanation as the best explanation.[74] This principle has been used by many later scientists to rule out in advance any supernatural causes since natural causes are thought to be less complex explanations. The theist responds by pointing out that often a supernatural explanation is less complex than naturalistic explanations.

THE SIXTEENTH CENTURY

Martin Luther (1483-1546) was the great German reformer who posted his famous 95 theses on the church door in Wittenberg. This was to protest what Luther felt were abuses in the Roman Catholic Church. Luther opposed the sale of indulgences and excessive church wealth. He denied the supremacy of the pope and considered the Bible alone to be the final authority for the church.

Though this work was mainly polemic in thrust, Luther also defended the doctrine of salvation by grace alone through faith alone in Christ alone.[75] Since salvation by grace is an essential doctrine of Christianity, its defense falls squarely in the field of apologetics.

John Calvin (1509-1564) was the famous Geneva reformer.[76] Like Luther, he broke from the Roman Catholic Church. He defended the scriptural doctrine of salvation only by God's grace through faith in Christ.[77] At a time when the Roman Catholic Church was elevating human effort in the attaining of salvation, Calvin, like Luther before him, stressed God's grace in salvation.[78]

Other great reformers include Huldreich Zwingli (1484-1531), William Tyndale (1494-1536), and John Knox (1514-1572). These men primarily defended the sole authority of the scriptures and salvation by grace through faith.[79]

THE SEVENTEENTH CENTURY

Rene Descartes (1596-1650) was a Roman Catholic philosopher.[80] He decided that something was not worth believing unless one could be certain about it.[81] He decided to reject any beliefs that could be doubted. In this way, he would attempt to find a belief that could not be doubted. This belief would be his point of certainty. From this belief, he would attempt to build an entire system of thought.[82]

As Descartes searched for this starting point, he began to doubt more and more beliefs. He became skeptical about all things. Finally, he found what he believed to be this point of certainty. For, the more he doubted, the more he became certain of the existence of the doubter (himself). Descartes coined his famous phrase "Cogito ergo sum" (I think, therefore I am).

From the starting point of his own existence, he attempted to build his system of thought. Descartes utilized Anselm's ontological argument for God's existence, as well as cosmological type arguments.[83] Though Descartes' goal was to defend the Christian faith, his effort ironically backfired in the history of western thought. For, if Descartes was correct and everything could be known through reason alone, what need is there for revelation from God? The extreme rationalism of Descartes eventually led to modernism—the attempt to find all truth through unaided human reason and the rejection of the possibility of divine revelation.

Blaise Pascal (1623-1662) was a great French thinker like Descartes, though their views had little in common. Pascal died while working on a defense of Christianity which was later published in its incomplete form as Pensees (Thoughts).[84] Pascal argued that human reason is fallen and, thus, tainted. Therefore, Pascal rejected the traditional arguments for God's existence. Man cannot reason to God. He concluded that faith is needed if man is to know God. Pascal did not deny that man is rational, but he rejected the idea that man is merely a rational being. There is more to man than his reason: man has a will; he has emotions; he knows some things by intuition. Man is a complex being; there are numerous factors that influence his reasoning.

Pascal argued that all men know they will die and that they are wretched. Yet, men choose to divert their attention from these things through recreation. By emphasizing man's need for God, Pascal pleaded with men to admit their fallen condition and to seek God with all their hearts.

Pascal was willing to provide historical evidences for the truth of Christianity. He used fulfilled prophecies of the Bible, the history of the Jewish nation, and the resurrection of Christ from the dead as evidence for the Christian faith.

Pascal is famous for his "wager" argument for God's existence. He reasoned that since the odds for and against God's existence are even, we cannot reason to God. We must use our will. We must either choose God or reject Him. Pascal concluded that if we wager that God exists and we find that He does in fact exist, we gain eternal happiness. But if God exists and we reject Him, we have lost everything. On the other hand, if God does not exist, we would still lose nothing by wagering that He does. Pascal stated that when a person wagers on God, he will either win or lose. If the person loses, he loses nothing. But if the person wins, he wins everything.

Therefore, the wise man will wager that God exists.[85] There is everything to gain and nothing to lose by wagering on God. Pascal's wager is not a rational argument for God's existence. Instead, Pascal is attempting to persuade his readers that it is reasonable to seek God in this life, and it is foolish to live like He does not exist. For, if we seek God with all our hearts, we will find Him.

Gottfried Wilhelm Leibniz (1646-1716) was a German Protestant.[86] Due to his extreme confidence in the abilities of human reason, he made use of the ontological argument for God's existence.[87] Leibniz also utilized the cosmological argument for God's existence.[88] He rested his form of this argument on the principle of sufficient reason. This principle states that everything that exists needs an explanation or reason for its existence. Dependent beings, such as human beings, need explanations outside of themselves for their existence. For example, one's existence cannot be explained without reference to his parents, the food that he eats, the air that he breathes, and so on. Leibniz concluded that eventually one must arrive at a Being which is totally independent. This Being contains within itself the reason for its own existence. Leibniz reasoned that if there is no such Being, then there is no ultimate explanation for the existence of dependent beings.

Leibniz disagreed with Augustine and Aquinas concerning the problem of evil. Leibniz reasoned that this is the best of all possible worlds, and that God could not create a world without evil. Most Christian thinkers have rejected Leibniz's speculation on the problem of evil, for Leibniz attributes evil to the creation, rather than to the Fall.

Baruch Spinoza (1623-1677) was a Jewish philosopher.[89] Although he was a proponent of the ontological argument, he used it in an attempt to prove the existence of an impersonal God. Spinoza was a pantheist—he believed that the universe is God.[90] In this way, he argued against the God of the Bible.

Spinoza believed that the science of his day had proven that the laws of nature could not be violated. Since he viewed miracles as violations of the laws of nature, he considered miracles impossible.[91] Up to that point in history, scholars had for the most part assumed the Bible to be a reliable document. However, from Spinoza on, many thinkers began to question the reliability and authenticity of the Bible. Human reason became the ultimate authority. It stood above the Bible as its judge. Men began to decide which portions of the Bible were inaccurate. Spinoza was the forerunner of the eighteenth century thinkers who were extremely critical of the veracity of the scriptures.

Spinoza dealt a devastating blow to Christian apologetics. If apologetics was ever to be revived, it must place more emphasis on scientific and historical evidences (the two areas thought to disprove the claims of Christianity).

THE EIGHTEENTH CENTURY

David Hume (1711-1776) was a Scottish philosopher and skeptic.[92] He was extremely skeptical about all areas of life. He was an empiricist, believing that truth could be found only through the five senses. Therefore, he believed that it was impossible to prove the existence of the self. He questioned the principle of causality (which forms the basis for the cosmological argument) since it could not be proven through sense experience. This principle states that every effect needs an adequate cause. Since Hume doubted this principle, he questioned the validity of the traditional arguments for God's existence (although he did give some weight to the teleological argument).[93] Following in the footsteps of Spinoza, Hume also questioned the possibility of miracles. He, like Spinoza, considered miracles violations of natural laws. Hume believed that the wise man bases his decisions upon the evidence. Since natural laws are based upon the uniform experience of mankind, the wise man will never believe in miracles.

Immanuel Kant (1724-1804) was a German philosopher. He taught that the thing in itself cannot be known by man. All man can know is the thing as it appears to him.[94] Man cannot know objective reality; all he can know is his own subjective views about reality. Kant's view took Christianity outside the realm of the objectively verifiable. He claimed that the traditional arguments for God's existence were flawed. Still, he felt that the moral nature of man made it practical to assume God's existence. For if there is no God, then there can be no after-life and no rewards. Therefore, in order to make sense of man's moral nature, we must posit the existence of God.[95] Although the moral argument was to become an effective tool for Christian apologists, the damage Kant had done far outweighed the good. Hegel and Kierkegaard would later pick up where Kant left off. They would inflict Christian apologetics with more serious wounds.

William Paley (1743-1805) was the Archdeacon of Carlisle. Despite the widespread skepticism of his day, he was an aggressive defender of the Christian faith. He wrote several apologetic works. His most famous contribution to Christian thought was his teleological argument for God's existence.

Paley's teleological argument is called the "watchmaker."[96] In this argument, Paley reasoned that if one found a watch in the wilderness, he would have to conclude that there must have been a watchmaker who designed it. Even if he had never seen a watch before, one would recognize the obvious design, order, and complexity of the watch and conclude that it was designed. Paley then asks his readers to consider the design in the universe and conclude with him that it also needs an intelligent Designer.

THE NINETEENTH CENTURY

Georg Wilhelm Friedrich Hegel (1770-1831) was a German philosopher who also dealt a devastating blow to Christian apologetics. Up to his day, men had viewed reality in terms of antithesis (opposites).[97] If something was true, its opposite must be false. Mankind accepted this law of non-contradiction. However, things began to change with Hegel.

Hegel accepted the view of the ancient Greek philosopher Heraclitus.[98] Heraclitus believed that every-thing is changing; nothing remains the same. Change was viewed by Heraclitus as the fundamental feature of reality.

Hegel saw this change as a dialectical process; real-ity is progressively developing through a threefold process. This process consists of a thesis which is followed by its antithesis (its opposite, a contradiction of the thesis), and then by a synthesis (the reconciling of the two opposites).[99] Therefore, in Hegel's philosophy, truth is relative. Contradictions can be reconciled. In short, the idea of abso-lute truth was discarded in Hegelian thought.

The result of this view upon Christian apologetics is obvious. The defense of the truth becomes futile because contradictions or opposites can both be true. Much of mod-ern philosophy is based upon this denial of absolutes, despite the fact that the denial of absolute truth is self-refuting. For if the denial is true, then it would be an absolute truth.

Soren Kierkegaard (1813-1855) was a famous Danish philosopher who took modern thought one step beyond that of Hegel. Kierkegaard is known as the "father of modern existentialism." Existentialism is the philosophi-cal school that either denies or de-emphasizes objective meaning while elevating subjective feelings and beliefs to a position of primacy.

The existentialism of Kierkegaard did not deny the existence of objective truth. However, Kierkegaard viewed subjective truth as of greater importance. Truth is viewed as something personal, not merely propositional. One's subjective beliefs are of greater importance than the objective truth.[100]

Applying this line of thought to religion, Kierkegaard held that religious beliefs could not be defended. One accepts something as true by an act of the will, not by reason. One accepts a religious truth by a leap of blind faith into the nonrational realm.[101] Faith and reason are worlds apart. Never shall the two meet. This view is called fideism. Fideism is opposed to Christian apologetics. It teaches that the defending of one's religious beliefs is useless. The distaste for apologetics harbored by many contemporary theologians can be directly traced to a Kierkegaardian influence.

Charles Darwin (1809-1882) published his famous work The Origin of Species in 1859. In this work, he attempted to present evidence for his view of evolution called natural selection (survival of the fittest).[102] Darwin's theory of evolution denied any need for God as the designer of the universe. Instead, the impersonal laws of nature were proposed to explain the origin of first life and of complex life forms. Life was thought to have evolved from non-life. Complex life forms supposedly evolved from simple life forms.

Finally, modern man, who wanted so desperately to be free from God's rule over his life, had no intellectual need to see God as the designer of the universe.[103] Belief in God was viewed as anti- intellectual.

Ludwig Feuerbach (1804-1872) believed that only the material realm exists. He reasoned that only the objects of sense are real. Therefore, he concluded that God and all religious values were created by man's imagination.[104] God is the imaginary fulfillment of man's wishes to transcend his own nature. In short, God did not create man; man created God.

Friedrich Nietzsche (1844-1900) accepted the atheistic evolutionary theory. This German philosopher concluded that since "God is dead," all traditional values died with Him.[105] In other words, man has philosophically and scientifically outgrown the outdated myths of religion. Modern man now recognizes that God is nonexistent. But, if the God of the Bible does not exist, then the morality taught in the Bible is no longer relevant. Nietzsche called for a race of "supermen" who would have the courage to go "beyond good and evil" and create their own moral values.[106] He recommended that the "soft" values of Christianity be replaced with the "hard" values of the "supermen," for the soft values of Christianity stifled human creativity.

THE ATHEISTIC BIAS OF THE TWENTIETH CENTURY

By the start of the twentieth century the atheistic bias was so prevalent among "intellectuals" that it was thought that no educated person could be a Christian. Dialogue between orthodox Christians and secular leaders became almost nonexistent. Christian apologetics needed to be revived in the midst of this antagonistic climate. Scientists, philosophers, and historians had attacked the Bible so thoroughly in the nineteenth century that Christian apologetics would have to start once again from the ground floor.

THE TWENTIETH CENTURY

Liberal theology was extremely popular at the start of the twentieth century. Liberal theology denied the inspiration and inerrancy of the scriptures and salvation only through Christ. Jesus was reduced to merely a wise man. Liberalism stressed the universal brotherhood of all men, the basic goodness of man, and the possibility of achieving world peace through human effort. However, two world wars effectively crumbled the foundations of liberalism.

The American reaction against liberalism was seen in the emergence of fundamentalism. The fundamentalists defended the orthodox doctrines of the Christian faith. They held to the inspiration and inerrancy of the Bible, the deity and resurrection of Christ, and salvation only through Him. Leading fundamentalists were B. B. Warfield, H. C. G. Moule, and James Orr.[107] They published a work in 1909 listing an entire series of orthodox beliefs which they held. Though fundamentalism is still strong today, it has come under much attack and has been accused of being anti-intellectual. Therefore, many Christians who hold to the fundamentals of the faith today, would rather be called "evangelicals."

Karl Barth (1886-1968) wrote his commentary on Romans in 1919. This marked his break from liberalism. His theological school of thought is called Neo-orthodoxy. Barth held that man was sinful and that God was "wholly other" than man.[108] However, he kept many liberal assumptions. He viewed the Bible as a human book that contained errors. Rather than the Bible objectively being God's inspired word, Barth believed that it becomes God's Word to the individual when the individual is encountered by God at the moment of crisis.[109] In effect, Barth introduced a heavy existential emphasis into the professing church. The propositional truths of Scripture were questioned. All that mattered was one's own personal encounter with God. Therefore, Barth was an extreme fideist. The fideism of Barth is still prevalent in the church today.

Rudolf Bultmann (1884-1976) was also a Neo-orthodox theologian. He used a method called form criticism to find what he felt were the oral traditions behind the written scriptures. He removed the supposed "myths" from God's Word.[110]

Despite the decline of Neo-orthodoxy that began in the 1950s, in its place, more secular and humanistic types of theology began to emerge. Any Christian theology that denies the essentials of the faith will eventually redefine Christianity in terms of its own secular culture. This was fully actualized when the "God is dead" theologies (so called "Christian atheism") were introduced in the 1960s.[111] The lessons of history have taught the church that a "watered-down" Christianity is no Christianity at all. Christian apologists found themselves defending the faith not only against the attacks of anti-Christian thinkers, but against professing Christians as well.

Yet, in the midst of this madness, a British scholar named C. S. Lewis (1898-1963) was converted from atheism to Christianity in 1931. He then became the most famous defender of orthodox Christianity in the English-speaking world until his death.[112] His writings provide rational arguments for the existence of God, the possibility of miracles, and the truth of the Christian faith. He also attempted to answer the question as to how an all-good and all-powerful God could allow evil and human suffering. With Lewis, the revival of Christian apologetics had begun. Many defenders of the faith were to follow in his footsteps.

Frederick Copleston, a Roman Catholic scholar, defended God's existence in a debate against the famous British philosopher Bertrand Russell in 1948.[113] Copleston is also the author of the nine-volume work A History of Philosophy.

Gordon Clark (1902-1985) and Cornelius Van Til (1895-1987) popularized the presuppositional school of apologetics.[114] They presupposed Christianity to be true rather than arguing for it. However, their willingness to refute non-Christian belief systems was enough to separate presuppositionalism from fideism, for fideists are opposed to all apologetics. A fideist will neither provide evidence for Christianity, nor refute non-Christian beliefs.

Edward John Carnell (1919-1967) also presupposed the truth of Christianity when he did apologetics. But, unlike Clark and Van Til, he believed that one's presuppositions could be tested.[115] His apologetic method could be called verificational presuppositionalism. Francis Schaeffer (1912-1984) reached many "intellectual dropouts" with the gospel through his writings, films, and lectures.[116] He managed to present the gospel at a philosophical level which touched the hearts and minds of many thinkers who were disenchanted with modern thought. Schaeffer's approach to apologetics was much like that of Carnell.

John Warwick Montgomery is a Lutheran scholar who gained notoriety in the 1960s for his lectures, books, and debates in defense of the Christian faith. Montgomery focused primarily on historical evidences for the Christian faith.[117]

Walter Martin (1928-1989) established himself as the foremost authority on refuting non-Christian cults in 1965. It was then that his book The Kingdom of the Cults was published.[118]

Today, there are many articulate defenders of the faith. Battling on the front lines are Christian philosophers Norman Geisler, William Lane Craig, Gary Habermas, and J. P. Moreland, as well as theologian R. C. Sproul. Christian apologetics is clearly making a comeback.

ENDNOTES

[1] Tim Dowley, ed., *The History of Christianity*, 83.

[2] J. B. Lightfoot and J. R. Harmer, eds., *The Apostolic Fathers* (Grand Rapids: Baker Book House, 1984), 148, 156.

[3] Cairns, 68.

[4] Ibid.

[5] Lightfoot and Harmer, 156.

[6] Dowley, 94.

[7] Cairns, 68.

[8] Ibid., 75-76.

[9] Ibid., 110.

[10] Ibid.

[11] Ibid.

[12] Dowley, 112.

[13] Ibid.

[14] Ibid.

[15] Ibid., 107.

[16] Ibid.

[17] Ibid., 145.

[18] Cairns, 134.

[19] Dowley, 149.

[20] Ibid., 175.

[21] Ibid., 206.

[22] Ibid., 98.

[23] Ibid., 206.

[24] St. Augustine, *City of God,* 14.11., 22.1.

[25] Vernon J. Bourke, *Augustine's Quest of Wisdom* (Albany: Magi Books, 1993), 136.

[26] Geisler and Feinberg, 288.

[27] St. Augustine, *City of God,* 13.3.

[28] Gordon H. Clark, *Thales to Dewey* (Jefferson: Trinity Foundation, 1985), 243-246.

[29] Geisler and Feinberg, 93-94.

[30] St. Augustine, *City of God,* 11.6.; Confessions, 11.11-14.

[31] Dowley, 229.

[32] Ibid., 241.

[33] Everett F. Harrison, Baker's Dictionary of Theology (Grand Rapids: Baker Book House, 1960), 26.

[34] St. Anselm, *Proslogium and Monologium.*

[35] Craig, *Apologetics,* 62.

[36] R. C. Sproul, John Gerstner, and Arthur Lindsley, *Classical Apologetics* (Grand Rapids: Academie Books, 1984), 102.

[37] St. Anselm, *Cur Deus Homo.*

[38] Dowley, 288-289.

[39] Ibid.

[40] Copleston, *A History of Philosophy*, book 1, vol. 2, 295.

[41] Ibid., 296.

[42] Ibid.

[43] Ibid., 299.

[44] Ibid., 298.

[45] Dowley, 292.

[46] Norman L. Geisler, *Thomas Aquinas: An Evangelical Appraisal* (Grand Rapids: Baker Book House, 1991), 86.

[47] Ibid.

[48] Ibid.

[49] Ibid., 87.

[50] Norman L. Geisler and Winfried Corduan, *Philosophy of Religion* (Grand Rapids: Baker Book House, 1988), 127.

[51] Copleston, *A History of Philosophy*, book 1, vol. 2, 338-339.

[52] *St. Thomas Aquinas, Summa Theologiae.* ed. Timothy McDermott. (Westminster: Christian Classics, 1989), 12-14.

[53] Geisler and Corduan, 158-159.

[54] Ibid., 159.

[55] Copleston, *A History of Philosophy*, book 1, vol. 2, 366-367.

[56] Geisler, *Thomas Aquinas*, 153-162.

[57] Ibid., 71-90.

[58] Ibid., 153-162, 123, 133, 97, 99.

[59] Ibid., 40.

[60] Ibid., 37.

[61] Ibid., 38.

[62] Ibid., 103.

[63] Ibid., 59-62..

[64] Copleston, *A History of Philosophy*, book 1, vol. 2, 251-252.

[65] Ibid., 252-253.

[66] Ibid., 255-256.

[67] Ibid., 256-257.

[68] Ibid., 262-265.

[69] Geisler and Corduan, 160-162.

[70] Sahakian, 116.

[71] Ibid., 172.

[72] Ibid., 188.

[73] Ibid., 346-348.

[74] Sahakian, 116.

[75] Martin Luther, *Commentary on Romans,* trans. J. Theodore Mueller (Grand Rapids: Kregel Publications, 1976), 76-80, 88-89.

[76] Dowley, 368-369.

[77] John Calvin, *On the Christian Faith: Selections From the Institutes, Commentaries, and Tracts.* ed. John T. McNeill (Indianapolis: The Bobbs-Merrill Company, 1957), 82-88.

[78] Ibid., 21-22.

[79] Dowley, 379, 390, 398.

[80] Ibid., 486-487.

[81] Sahakian, 135.

[82] Ibid.

[83] Geisler and Corduan, 127-131, 163.

[84] Blaise Pascal, *Pensees.* trans. by A. J. Krailsheimer. (London: Penguin Books, 1966).

[85] Craig, *Apologetics,* 33-36.

[86] Dowley, 489.

[87] Geisler and Corduan, 131-132.

[88] Ibid., 164-165.

[89] Dowley, 487-489.

[90] Geisler and Corduan, 132-133.

[91] Norman L. Geisler, *The Battle For the Resurrection* (Nashville: Thomas Nelson Publishers, 1989), 67.

[92] Dowley, 490-491.

[93] David Hume, *Dialogues Concerning Natural Religion.* ed. Henry D. Aiken. (New York: Hafner Publishing Company, 1948), 95.

[94] Gordon H. Clark, *Thales to Dewey,* 402.

[95] Geisler and Corduan, 109-110.

[96] Hick, ed., *The Existence of God*, 99-104.

[97] Francis A. Schaeffer, *The Complete Works of Francis A. Schaeffer.* Vol. 1. (Westchester: Crossway Books, 1982), 13-14.

[98] Sahakian, 190.

[99] Ibid., 191-192.

[100] Geisler and Feinberg, 46.

[101] Ibid.

[102] Sahakian, 225.

[103] Ibid.

[104] Ibid., 202.

[105] Ibid., 231.

[106] Ibid.

[107] Dowley, 611-612.

[108] Cairns, 444-445.

[109] Ibid.

[110] Ibid., 446.

[111] Ibid., 446-447.

[112] Dowley, 621.

[113] Hick, ed., *The Existence of God,* 167-191.

[114] Gordon R. Lewis, *Testing Christianity's Truth Claims* (Lanham: University Press of America, 1990), 100-150

[115] Ibid., 176-284.

[116] Cairns, 454.

[117] John Warwick Montgomery, *History and Christianity* (Minneapolis: Bethany Book House, 1965).

[118] Walter Martin, *The Kingdom of the Cults* (Minneapolis: Bethany Book House, 1985).

CHAPTER 4

TRUTH AND KNOWLEDGE

Biblical Christianity makes truth claims. The apostle Paul refers to God's Word as "the word of truth" (2 Timothy 2:15), and Jesus states concerning the teachings of His Father: "Thy word is truth" (John 17:17).

Since Christianity makes truth claims, believers must acknowledge the existence of absolute truths (i.e., truths that are true for all people, at all times, and in all places). The rejection of absolute truth is not compatible with the Christian world view. Therefore, the Christian apologist must be ready to defend the existence of absolute truths.

PREMODERNISM

Western culture was once dominated by the premodern mindset. The premodern period and mindset covers a time frame that extends from ancient Greek philosophy through the medieval period. Though the beliefs that were held during this long period of time varied greatly, a common set of assumptions can be found. During premodern times, truth was believed to be absolute, and as that which corresponded to reality. There was a confidence that human reason could find truth since the universe made sense. There was thought to be a purpose for the universe and a pattern to history. There was a common belief in the real existence of the physical universe, as well as a shared acknowledgement of a reality beyond the realm of the five senses.[1] Obviously, the Christian world view fit very nicely within the premodern mindset.

MODERNISM

Eventually, premodernism gave rise to modernism. Many of the convictions of premodernism were retained in modern thought; however, the notion of a reality beyond the realm of the senses was rejected.

Modernism can trace its roots to the French philosopher Rene Descartes (1596-1650).[2] Although he professed to be a Christian, Descartes chose to doubt everything until he could find something that could not be doubted. This would be a point of certainty from which he could deduce all other knowledge. The more Descartes doubted, the more he became aware of the existence of the doubter (i.e., himself). Descartes stated "cogito ergo sum" (I think, therefore I am). From this foundation, Descartes sought to find all truth through human reason alone.[3]

Thus, the modern project began. Modernism was characterized by this attempt to find all truth with certainty through unaided human reason. But, if man through unaided human reason could find truth, then what need is there for revelation from God? The supernatural realm was eventually rejected, and the dominant perspective of western culture became characterized by an atheistic mindset and a confidence in the power of unaided human reason to find truth and solve the problems which mankind faced.[4] Hence, modernism is no friend of the Christian world view.

POSTMODERNISM

The modern attempt to find truth and solve man's greatest problems failed. Newtonian physics, which was produced by the modern mindset, proved inadequate as an explanation for the workings of the universe.[5] In short, the modern experiment ended in disaster. Although many people continue to think along modernistic lines, modernism died as the dominant intellectual climate of western culture.

Modernism's failure, rather than leading to a return to premodern thought forms, has led to postmodernism. Postmodernism is characterized by the rejection of absolute truth and the loss of confidence in human reason as a means to discover "truth."[6] Since postmodern thinking is becoming more widespread, the Christian apologist must be able to defend the existence of absolute truth and man's ability to know it.

SCHAEFFER'S LINE OF DESPAIR

The Christian thinker Francis Schaeffer (1912-1984) argued that contemporary man had fallen below what he called "the line of despair."[7] By this he meant that contemporary man has given up any hope of ever finding absolute truth. Schaeffer identified three thinkers whose ideas led to this loss of absolutes: Immanuel Kant (1724-1804), Georg Wilhelm Friedrich Hegel (1770-1831), and Soren Kierkegaard (1813-1855).

Immanuel Kant argued that we can know reality as it appears to us (phenomena), not reality as it is (noumena).[8] The a priori categories of the mind read order into reality, not an order that is already there. Hence, according to Kant, man cannot know reality as it is.

Hegel defined truth as the unfolding world process. History unfolds in the form of a thesis which is opposed by its contrary—the antithesis. The thesis and antithesis are eventually synthesized to produce a new truth.[9] Before

Hegel, the thesis was viewed as true, while the antithesis was considered false. Now, due to Hegel's influence, many believe that two contradictory statements can be synthesized. Hence, the law of noncontradiction (A cannot equal non-A at the same time and in the same way) is denied.

Kierkegaard emphasized the subjective nature of truth and de-emphasized the objective nature of truth. He believed that meaning, truth, and values cannot be found in the realm of reason. To find meaning, truth, and values we must take a leap of blind faith into the nonrational realm. Kierkegaard argued that truth is found by a passionate act of the will, and not through reason.[10]

According to Schaeffer, the influence of these three thinkers has caused contemporary man to either deny the reality of absolute truths or at least give up the search for absolute truths. If Schaeffer is correct in his assessment of contemporary man, than the Christian must defend the concept of absolute truth before proclaiming the gospel, for the gospel is "true truth," (i.e., true in the traditional sense; absolutely true; true for all people, at all times, in all places). The gospel is not merely true in a subjective sense.

CLARK'S REFUTATION OF NON-CHRISTIAN THEORIES OF KNOWLEDGE

Christian philosopher Gordon Clark (1902-1985) argued that all non-Christian theories of knowledge fail. Clark discussed empiricism, rationalism, and irrationalism in his writings.

Empiricism is the attempt to find truth through the five senses alone. This school of thought believes "that all knowledge begins in sense experience."[11] Clark agrees with David Hume (1711-1776) in his observation that the principle of cause and effect, the existence of external bodies, and the reality of internal selves could not be proven through sense data alone. Therefore, Hume admitted that his own empiricism inevitably led to skepticism.[12] Clark emphasized that there is a large gap between basic sense experience and the propositional, rational conclusions arrived at by empiricists.[13] Sense data (the facts of experience) do not come with their own built-in interpretation. Rational conclusions cannot come from sense experience alone. Empiricism, therefore, fails as a truth-finding method.

Rationalism is the attempt to find truth through reason alone. Clark was not impressed by rationalism as a means to find truth. Rationalism has historically led to several contradictory conclusions (i.e., theism, pantheism, panentheism, and atheism).[14] Also, Clark stated that "rationalism does not produce first principles out of something else: the first principles are innate."[15] Clark argued that every philosophy, including rationalism, must presuppose its first principles.[16] Therefore, rationalism fails, for it cannot prove its own first principles through reason alone. At best, rationalism can show us that the contradictory is false; but, it cannot show us that the non-contradictory is true.

It should also be noted that if we attempt to find truth by combining rationalism and empiricism, Kant's dilemma resurfaces, for there is no way to guarantee that the rational categories of the mind rightly interpret sense data.

Clark reminds us that the philosophies of Hume, Kant, and Hegel have led to skepticism.[17] Since both empiricism and rationalism have failed, some thinkers have turned to irrationalism as the method of finding meaning in life. One such thinker was Soren Kierkegaard. Kierkegaard tried to find true meaning in life through a leap of blind faith.[18] Though Clark admitted the widespread influence of Kierkegaard's irrationalism on today's thinkers, Clark rejected irrationalism as a means to find truth. Clark reasoned that when a person rejects logic and accepts contradictions, his language and arguments become meaningless.[19] Therefore, irrationalism cannot be consistently defended.

After pointing out the inadequacy of human wisdom (i.e., empiricism, rationalism, and irrationalism), Clark argued that we must choose between skepticism and a word from God.[20] Clark then presupposed the existence of the rational God who has revealed Himself in Scripture as the first principle of his philosophical system.

CHRISTIAN RESPONSE #1:
TRUTH IS UNIVERSAL

Since postmodernists deny the reality of absolute or universal truth, a Christian response is needed. Postmodernists must be shown that the statement "there is no absolute truth" is a self-refuting statement.[21] For, if this statement is true, then it would be an absolute truth. But, then it would refute itself. In short, the statement cannot be true. Therefore, absolute truth must exist. There is no escaping this conclusion. However, even if absolute truth exists, how can we be confident that we can know this truth?

CHRISTIAN RESPONSE #2:
MAN CAN KNOW TRUTH

The Christian response to skepticism is threefold. First, Kant's dilemma is self-refuting. The statement, "we can know reality as it appears to us and not reality as it is," is itself a claim to know something about reality (i.e., that it cannot be known as it is). Therefore, Kant's dilemma must be false. It is possible for man to know reality as it is.

Second, skepticism is not an option, for skepticism is the suspending of all judgment. Yet, the skeptic does not suspend judgment about his skepticism. He is dogmatic about his skepticism. (The truth of the matter is this: humans must be dogmatic about something; there is no escape from some form of dogmatism.) Also, no one can live consistently with his skepticism, for even skeptics eat food. They do not suspend judgment about whether or not to eat.[22] Any world view that cannot be consistently lived should be abandoned.

Third, agnosticism, in its strongest form, fails. For the statement, "man cannot know," is itself a claim to know something (i.e., that man cannot know). Hence, it is a self-refuting statement, and, therefore, cannot be true.[23] But if the statement "man cannot know" is false, then the statement "man can know" must be true. Therefore, man is capable of knowing the truth. Man can know that he knows, even if he doesn't know how he knows.

THE NEED FOR A CHRISTIAN THEORY OF KNOWLEDGE

Since it is possible for man to know truth, we need to propose a Christian epistemology (theory of knowledge). I am convinced that, apart from the infinite/personal/rational God of theism, there is no guarantee that the categories of the mind enable us to know reality as it is. Schaeffer stated:

> It is not surprising that if a reasonable God created the universe and put me in it, he should also correlate the categories of my mind to fit that universe, simply because I have to live in it. . . . If this world is made the way the Judeo-Christian system says it is made, we should not be surprised that man should have categories of the mind to fit the universe in which he lives.[24]

The biblical creation account (Genesis 1:1, 26-27) teaches that we were created in the image of the rational God and, therefore, we are rational beings. It teaches that this same God also created the universe in which we live.

If we assume the truth of the biblical creation account, then it only makes sense that God fashioned the categories (the innate ideas) of the human mind in such a way so that we could use them to truly know the world in which we live. "In God's light, we see light" (Psalm 36:9). We can know our world because the infinite Knower has created us (finite knowers) in such a way that we can know the world He has created. If we reject the creation account (i.e., the existence of the infinite/rational/personal God), then the Kantian dilemma remains. And, since the Kantian dilemma is self-refuting, we have verification for our assumption of the biblical God. In short, without the biblical God, we are doomed to skepticism. But, once we assume the existence of the Biblical God, then real knowledge is a given. The existence of the biblical God explains man's ability to know truth.

The first principles of knowledge are the starting points in human thought and knowledge. Some of these first principles are the law of noncontradiction (A cannot equal non-A at the same time in the same way), the law of causality (every effect must have an adequate cause; non-being cannot cause being), the principle of analogy (similar effects have similar causes), and the basic reliability of sense perception. These first principles are self-evident truths; they are beyond reasonable doubt. Their denial is forced and temporary. They are actually undeniable. If we try to deny or disprove these first principles, we must use them in the denial or refutation.

Christian thinkers often view the relationship between the first principles and the human mind in different ways. At least three different Christian theories of knowledge have been proposed.

Augustine (354-430AD) promoted a theory of divine illumination. He accepted Plato's basic theory of knowledge since he believed that the first principles are eternal, unchanging ideas. But, unlike Plato (who believed we remember these ideas due to past lives), Augustine believed that these eternal ideas exist in the mind of God, and that man cannot perceive these eternal ideas unless his mind is illuminated by God.[25]

Thomas Aquinas (1225-1274AD) was an adherent of Aristotle's theory of knowledge. Aquinas believed that man begins life with his mind as a blank slate, and that all knowledge comes through sense experience. Aquinas rejected the notion that man is created with innate ideas; rather, he believed that God created us with the innate ability to discover the first principles of knowledge through sense experience. Aquinas stated that "everything in the mind was first in the senses except the mind itself."[26]

Christian philosopher Stuart Hackett believes that God created man with innate ideas. The first principles of knowledge were implanted in our minds at creation; they are innate—man is born with these ideas in his mind.[27]

CONCLUSION

Christians reject relativism, for there is absolute truth. Christians reject agnosticism, for man can know truth. Only theism (the belief in a personal God) adequately explains why man is able to know truth.

One final thing needs to be noted in this chapter. Though the Christian world view necessitates propositional truth (statements of truth), there is more to Christianity than propositional truths (i.e., doctrinal creeds). True Christianity is also concerned with a personal saving encounter with the God of the Bible through Jesus Christ. However, before someone can enter into a personal relationship with the true Jesus of the Bible, he must believe the right propositional truths about this Jesus to ensure that he is not guilty of worshiping a false Jesus. In other words, though we must have the right beliefs about God, that alone is not enough. When we find the true God, we must then enter into a personal relationship of love and trust with Him in order to be saved (Matthew 11:28; John 3:16; 17:3).

ENDNOTES

[1] Millard J. Erickson, *Postmodernizing the Faith* (Grand Rapids: Baker Book House, 1997), 15.

[2] Stanley Grenz, *A Primer on Postmodernism* (Eerdmans Publishing Company: Grand Rapids, 1996), 63.

[3] Ibid., 64.

[4] Erickson, *Postmodernizing the Faith*, 16-17.

[5] Grenz, 50.

[6] Erickson, *Postmodernizing the Faith*, 118-19.

[7] Schaeffer, *Complete Works*, vol. 1, 8.

[8] Ibid., vol. 5, 177-178.

[9] Ibid., vol. 1, 13-14.

[10] Ibid., vol. 1, 14-16.

[11] Geisler and Feinberg, 431.

[12] Gordon H. Clark, *Three Types of Religious Philosophy*, (Jefferson: The Trinity Foundation, 1989), 71, 76-78.

[13] Ibid., 91.

[14] Ibid., 56.

[15] Ibid., 117-118.

[16] Ibid.

[17] Gordon H. Clark, *Religion, Reason, and Revelation* (Jefferson: The Trinity Foundation, 1986), 62.

[18] Clark, *Three Types of Religious Philosophy*, 101-105.

[19] Ibid., 114.

[20] Gordon H. Clark, *Thales to Dewey*, 534.

[21] Geisler, *Christian Apologetics*, 135.

[22] Ibid., 20-21, 133-135.

[23] Ibid., 26-27, 142.

[24] Schaeffer, vol. 1, 335.

[25] Bourke, *Augustine's Quest of Wisdom,* 79, 117, 136.

[26] Geisler, *Thomas Aquinas,* 71-90.

[27] Stuart C. Hackett, T*he Resurrection of Theism* (Chicago: Moody Press, 1957), 64.

CHAPTER 5

THE CUMULATIVE CASE FOR GOD

INTRODUCTION

My case for the existence of a personal, infinite God does not rest on the validity of one sole argument. Instead, I have chosen to utilize a cumulative case for God. This cumulative case will examine nine different aspects of human experience that are more adequately explained by theism (the belief in a personal God) than by atheism (the rejection of the belief in a personal God). The thesis I seek to defend is as follows: it is more reasonable to be a theist than it is to be an atheist.

The God of theism is the eternal uncaused Cause of all else that exists. This Being is personal (i.e., a moral and intelligent being) and unlimited in all His attributes. This Being is separate from His creation (transcendent), but He is also involved with it (immanent).

1) THE BEGINNING OF THE UNIVERSE

This argument is called the kalaam cosmological

argument for God's existence. Saint Bonaventure utilized this argument.[1] William Lane Craig and J. P. Moreland are two modern proponents of it.[2] This argument is as follows: 1) whatever began to exist must have a cause, 2) the universe began to exist, 3) therefore, the universe had a cause.

Premise #1 uses the law of causality—non-being cannot cause being. In other words, from nothing, nothing comes. Since nothing is nothing, it can do nothing. Therefore, it can cause nothing. Hence, whatever began to exist needs a cause for its existence.

Premise #2 contends that the universe had a beginning. Scientific evidence for the beginning of the universe includes the second law of thermodynamics (energy deterioration) and the Big Bang Model. The second law of thermodynamics is one of the most firmly established laws of modern science. It states that the amount of usable energy in a closed system is running down. This means that someday in the finite future all the energy in the universe will be useless (unless there is intervention from "outside" the universe). In other words, if left to itself, the universe will have an end. But if the universe is going to have an end, it had to have a beginning. At one time, in the finite past, all the energy in the universe was usable. Since the universe is winding down, it must have been wound up. The universe is not eternal; it had a beginning. Since it had a beginning, it needs a cause, for from nothing, nothing comes.

It should also be noted that, due to energy deterioration, if the universe is eternal it would have reached a state of equilibrium in which no change is possible an infinite amount of time ago. All of the universe's energy would already have been used up. Obviously, this is not the case. Therefore, the universe had a beginning.

The Big Bang Model also indicates that the universe had a beginning. In 1929, astronomer Edwin Hubble discovered that the universe is expanding at the same rate in all directions. As time moves forward the universe is growing apart. But this means that if we go back in time the physical universe would get smaller and smaller. Eventually, if we go back far enough in the past, the entire universe would be what scientists call "a point of infinite density" or "a point of dimensionless space." However, if something is infinitely dense, it is non-existent, for existent things can only be finitely small. The same can be said for points of dimensionless space. If a point has no dimensions, it is non-existent for it takes up no space. Therefore, if the Big Bang Model is correct, it shows that the universe began out of nothing a finite time ago.

There have been two main attempts to refute the beginning of the universe. The first is called the steady-state model. This view holds that the universe never had a beginning. Instead, it always existed in the same state. Because of the mounting evidence for the Big Bang Model, this view has been abandoned my most of its adherents.

The second attempt to evade the beginning of the universe is called the oscillating model. This model teaches that, at some point during the universe's expansion, gravity will halt the expansion and pull everything back together again. From that point there will be another big bang. This process will be repeated over and over again throughout all eternity. However, the oscillating model fails. First, there is no known principle of physics that would reverse the collapse of the universe and cause another big bang. Second, current scientific research has shown that the universe is not dense enough for gravity to pull it back together again. And third, even if it could be proven that several big bangs have occurred, the second law of thermodynamics would still require that there was a first big bang.

Many scientists accept the beginning of the universe, but believe that it does not need a cause. The evidence proposed by these scientists consists of speculation dealing with quantum physics (the study of subatomic particles). Appeal is made to Heisenberg's Principle of Indeterminacy in order to claim that quantum particles pop into existence out of nothing, entirely without a cause. However, Heisenberg's Principle does not necessitate such an absurd interpretation. Simply because scientists cannot presently find the causes does not mean that the causes do not exist. All that Heisenberg's Principle states is that scientists are presently unable to accurately predict where a specific subatomic particle will be at a given time. If this principle proved that events can occur without causes then this would destroy one of the pillars of modern science—the principle of causality (every event must have an adequate cause). It seems obvious to me that the principle of causality is on firmer epistemological ground than the belief that things can pop into existence without a cause. Non-being cannot cause being. If the universe had a beginning, then it needs a cause. Besides this scientific evidence there is also philosophical evidence for the beginning of the universe. If the universe is eternal, then there would be an actual infinite number of events in time. However, as Zeno's paradoxes have shown, it is impossible to traverse an actual infinite set of points. If we assume the existence of an infinite amount of actual points between two locations, then we can never get from location A to location B, since no matter how many points we have traversed, there will still be an infinite number of points left. If the universe is eternal, then there must exist an actual infinite set of events in the past, but then it would be impossible to reach the present moment. Since the present moment has been reached, there cannot be an actual infinite set of events in the past. There could only be a finite number. Therefore, there had to be a first event. Hence, the universe had a beginning.

It should also be noted that if it is possible for an actual infinite set to exist outside of a mind, contradictions and absurdities would be generated. To illustrate this point, let us look at two infinite sets. Set A consists of all numbers, both odd and even. Set B contains only all the odd numbers. Set A and Set B are equal since they both have an infinite number of members. Still, Set A has twice the number of members as Set B since Set A contains both odd and even numbers, while Set B contains only odd numbers. It is a clear contradiction to say that Set A and Set B have an equal amount of members, while Set A has twice as many members as Set B. Therefore, actual infinite sets cannot exist outside the mind. Actual sets existing outside the mind can only be potentially infinite, not actually infinite. These sets can be added to indefinitely; still, we will never reach an actual infinite by successive addition. Therefore, the universe cannot have an infinite number of events in the past. The universe had a beginning.

Since the universe had to have a beginning, it had to have a cause. For from nothing nothing comes. But if the universe needs a cause, what if the cause of the universe also needs a cause? Could we not have an infinite chain of causes and effects stretching backwards in time throughout all eternity? Obviously, the answer is no, for we have already shown that an actual infinite set existing outside of a mind is impossible. Therefore, an infinite chain of causes and effects is also impossible. There had to be a first uncaused Cause of the universe. This uncaused Cause would be eternal, without beginning or end. Only eternal and uncaused existence can ground the existence of the universe.

In short, there are only four possible explanations as to why the universe exists. First, the universe could be an eternal chain of causes and effects. Second, the universe could have popped into existence out of nothing without a cause. Third, the universe could merely be an illusion. And, fourth, the universe could have been caused to come into existence by an eternal, uncaused Cause (i.e., God). I have provided strong evidence against the first and second options, as well as strong argumentation in favor of the fourth option. The third option is not a viable position, since it cannot be affirmed without contradiction. Those who claim the universe is an illusion usually contend that all of reality is one mind. However, the communicating of this view necessitates and assumes the existence of two or more minds. Hence, the statement that the universe is an illusion is self-refuting. Therefore, the most plausible explanation for the existence of the universe is that is has an uncaused Cause.

Several attributes of the uncaused Cause of the universe can be discovered through examination of the universe. Intelligent life exists in the universe. Since intelligence is a perfection found in the universe, the ultimate Cause of the universe must also be an intelligent Being, for intelligence cannot come from non-intelligence. No one has ever presented a reasonable explanation as to how intelligence could evolve from mindless nature.

Morality also exists in the universe, for without morality, there would be no such thing as right and wrong. However, the moral judgments we make show that we do believe there are such things as right and wrong. Still, nature is non-moral. No one holds a rock morally responsible for tripping him. There is no way that mere "molecules in motion" could produce moral values. Since nature is non-moral but morality exists in the universe, the Cause of the universe must be a moral Being.

The moral law is not invented by individuals, for one individual judges the actions of another. If morality is relative and subjective, then no one could call the actions of Adolph Hitler wrong. Nor could society be the cause of moral laws, since societies often pass judgment on one another (America and the Allies denounced the actions of Nazi Germany). Even world consensus fails to qualify for the source of moral values since the world consensus once held slavery to be morally defensible. Only an absolute moral Lawgiver who is qualitatively above man can be the Cause of a moral law that stands above man and judges his actions. This moral Lawgiver must be eternal and unchanging since we make moral judgments about the past (slavery, evil treatment of women). Therefore, the uncaused Cause of the universe must be an intelligent, moral Being. This means that God must be a personal Being.

2) THE CONTINUING EXISTENCE OF THE UNIVERSE

This argument for God's existence derives its substance from Thomas Aquinas' five ways to prove God's existence.[3] Experience shows us that limited, dependent beings exist. These limited, dependent beings need other beings for their continued existence. For example, I depend on air, water, and food to sustain my existence. However, adding limited, dependent beings will never give us an independent and unlimited whole. Therefore, the sum total of limited, dependent beings is itself limited and dependent. (If each individual part of a floor is wood, then the whole floor will be wood. Likewise, if each part of the universe is dependent, then the entire universe is dependent.) Hence, the ultimate Cause of the continuing existence of all limited, dependent beings must be unlimited and independent.

There cannot be two or more unlimited and independent beings since, if there were, they would limit one another's existence, but then they would not be unlimited. Therefore, there can only be one unlimited and independent Being.

This Being must have all its attributes in an unlimited way. Otherwise, it would not be an unlimited Being. This Being must be all-powerful, for He is the source of all the power in the universe. No other power can limit Him. He is eternal for He is not limited by time. He is everywhere present since He is not limited by space. He is immaterial since He is not limited by matter. This Being must be all-good since He is not limited by evil. He must also be all-knowing since He is not limited by ignorance.

Since mindless nature works towards goals (such as acorns always becoming oak trees and not something else), there must be an intelligent Designer overseeing natural processes. Without intelligent design, nature's processes would be left to chance. There would be no orderly patterns that could be described as natural laws. Therefore, this infinite and independent Being, whom all finite and dependent beings depend upon for their continued existence, must be an intelligent Being.

3) THE DESIGN & ORDER FOUND IN THE UNIVERSE

The order, design, and complexity found in the universe strongly imply that the universe is not a random, chaotic throwing together of atoms; rather, it is the product of intelligent design. And, as the product of intelligent design, it necessitates the existence of an intelligent Designer.

Contemporary scientists have found numerous evidences for design in the universe.[4] A few examples will suffice. First, the slightest variation in the expansion rate of the universe would render the universe incapable of sustaining life.

Second, British scientists Hoyle and Wickramasinghe estimated that the chances of life evolving from the random shuffling of organic molecules is virtually zero. They calculated that there is only one chance in 1020 to form a single enzyme, and just one chance in 1040,000 to produce the approximately 2,000 enzymes that exist. However, Hoyle and Wickramasinghe point out that the production of enzymes is only one step in the generation of life. Therefore, they concluded there must be some type of Cosmic Intelligence to explain the origin of life.[5] Hoyle compared the probability of life spontaneously generating from non-life as equivalent to the chances of a tornado producing a Boeing 747 from a junkyard.[6]

The cell is the basic unit of life. The DNA molecule of a single-celled animal contains enough complex information to fill one volume of an encyclopedia.[7] An explosion in a print shop will never produce one volume of an encyclopedia. That amount of information necessitates an intelligent cause. Also, the human brain contains more genetic information than the world's largest libraries.8 There is no way that this amount of information could be produced by mere chance. Intelligent intervention is needed.

Third, astrophysicist Hugh Ross listed twenty-five narrowly defined parameters that the universe had to have in order for life to be possible.[9] Ross also pointed out thirty-two narrowly defined parameters for life concerning the earth, its moon, its sun, and its galaxy.[10] For instance, if the distance between the earth and the sun was to differ by just two percent in either direction, no life on earth would be possible.[11] These parameters for life on earth clearly show evidence of design and purpose. The theistic hypothesis of intelligent design is obviously more plausible than the atheistic hypothesis of random chance.

4) THE POSSIBILITY OF HUMAN KNOWLEDGE

The theist claims to know something (i.e., that God exists), and the atheist claims to know something (i.e., that God does not exist). Even the agnostic claims to know something (i.e., that the supposed evidence for God's existence is insufficient). However, it seems to me that only theism (the belief in a personal God) justifies the possibility of human knowledge. For instance, Immanuel Kant argued that man could only know reality as it appeared to him and not reality as it is. Atheism and agnosticism offer no good reason why we should assume that the gap between reality and appearance can be bridged. However, theism entails the doctrine that a rational God created man in His image (i.e., a rational being) and a coherent universe so that through reason man could find out about the universe in which he lives. Remove the rational God of theism from the equation, and the basis for human knowledge appears to crumble.

5) THE REALITY OF UNIVERSAL, UNCHANGING TRUTHS

The denial of absolute truth is self-refuting, for if the statement "there is no absolute truth" is true, then it would be an absolute truth. Complete agnosticism is also self-refuting, for to say that man cannot know truth is a claim to know this "truth." Therefore, there is absolute truth and it is possible for man to know truth.

Some truths are universal, unchanging, and eternal. An example of this would be the mathematical truth "1 + 1 = 2." We do not invent mathematical truths—we discover them. This also applies to the laws of logic (the law of non-contradiction, the law of excluded middle, the law of identity, etc.). These truths stand above human minds and judge human minds. For instance, if we add 1 + 1 and we conclude with 3, the eternal truth that 1 + 1 = 2 will declare us wrong. However, Augustine argued that it is not likely that human, fallible minds are the ultimate cause of universal, unchanging, eternal truths. Augustine concluded that an unchanging, eternal Mind must be the ultimate source of these truths.[12]

Atheism has no basis for eternal, unchanging truths. If atheism is "true," then there may have been a time when 1 + 1 equaled 3. There may also have been a time when torturing innocent babies was good. In fact, if atheism is true, there may have been a time when the statement "God exists" was true.

6) THE EXISTENCE OF ABSOLUTE MORAL VALUES

We all make moral value judgments when we call the actions of another person wrong. When we do this, we appeal to a moral law. This moral law could not originate with each individual, for then we could not call the actions of another person, such as Adolph Hitler, wrong.

The moral law is not a creation of each society, for then one society cannot call the actions of another society, such as Nazi Germany, wrong. The moral law does not come from a world consensus, for world consensus is often mistaken. The world once thought that the earth was flat, the sun revolved around the earth, and slavery was morally acceptable. Appealing to society or world consensus will never give us an adequate cause for the moral law and the moral judgments we make. Appealing to society or world consensus only quantitatively adds men and women. What we need is a moral law qualitatively above man. This moral law must be eternal and unchanging so that we can condemn the actions of the past (i.e., slavery, the holocaust, etc.).

The moral law qualitatively above man is not descriptive of the way things are (as is the case with natural laws). The moral law must be prescriptive—it describes the way things ought to be.[13] Prescriptive laws need a Prescriber. Therefore, a moral Lawgiver must exist, and this Lawgiver must be eternal and unchanging.

We are accountable to this moral Lawgiver that stands above all mankind. Atheist Sigmund Freud failed miserably in his attempt to explain the universal experience of guilt.[14] I believe that the best explanation for the guilt we all experience is the fact that we know we stand guilty before a righteous and holy God. Therefore, when we make moral value judgments, whether it involves self-judgment (a guilty conscience) or judgment of another person, we appeal to a transcendent objective moral law. This is a strong indication that there exists a transcendent moral Lawgiver.

7) THE ABSURDITY OF LIFE WITHOUT GOD

Each of us thirsts for something more; life on earth never fully satisfies. It is my contention that only the God of the Bible can fully satisfy man's deepest needs. What hope can an atheist offer mankind? People on their deathbeds don't usually call an atheist to comfort them—normally a preacher or a priest is summoned. Even if an atheist could guarantee us seventy years of happiness, what good would that be when compared with the eternity of non-existence that follows? If there is no God who sits enthroned, then Hitler will not be punished for his evil deeds, and Mother Theresa will not be rewarded for her generous works of charity. If there is no God, then a million years from now what would it matter if you were a Hitler or a Mother Theresa? What difference would it make?

Does life have any ultimate meaning if there is no God? If nonexistence is what awaits us, can we really make sense of life? You live and then you die. There are no eternal consequences. Hitler and Mother Theresa have the same destiny. We all finish our meaningless journeys in total nothingness. The famous atheist Bertrand Russell wrote:

> That man is the product of causes which had no prevision of the end they were achieving; that his origin, his growth, his hopes and fears, his loves and his beliefs, are but the outcome of accidental collocations of atoms; that no fire, no heroism, no intensity of thought and feeling, can preserve an individual life beyond the grave; that all the labors of the ages, all the devotion, all the inspiration, all the noonday brightness of human genius, are destined to extinction in the vast death of the solar system, and that the whole temple of man's

achievement must inevitably be buried beneath the debris of a universe in ruins . . .[15]

Immediately following this statement, Russell referred to his atheistic philosophy as "the firm foundation of unyielding despair."[16] Without God, life is without meaning.

However, if there is a God, then there is hope. The God of the Bible guarantees the defeat of evil and the triumph of good. He guarantees that Hitler will receive his punishment and Mother Theresa will receive her reward. God gives life meaning, for how we choose to live our lives on earth brings eternal consequences. God is our reason to be optimistic about the future. Only He can overcome our fear of death; only He can defeat evil. Without God, meaningless existence is all we face. Without God, there is no hope.

8) RESPECT FOR HUMAN LIFE

If atheism is true, then man is mere molecules in motion. He has no greater value than the animals. In fact, human life would be no more sacred than the existence of a rock. Yet, we act as if human life has more value than the life of animals or the existence of rocks. If the material universe is all there is, then man is just a material part of the universe. There seems to be no basis from which to argue for human rights or the sanctity of human life. Even our founding fathers (who were not always consistent with their ideals) grounded their view of unalienable human rights in their belief that "all men are created equal." I propose that the most reasonable explanation for our common conception of human rights is the biblical teaching that human life has value since we were created in God's image.

9) THE EXISTENCE OF EVIL (IT'S CAUSE & ULTIMATE DEFEAT)

Atheists often argue that the existence or amount of

evil in the world disproves the existence of the God of the Bible. I see two difficulties with this view. These difficulties cause the argument against God's existence from evil to backfire into an argument for God's existence.[17]

The first difficulty is that the atheist has no explanation for evil within his world view. If the atheist accepts the existence of evil, he must define what it is. If he denies the existence of evil, then he has no basis upon which to call any action evil. Evil can be defined as the perversion or corruption of that which is good. However, for good to be objectively real its existence must be grounded in something ultimately good. In other words, if the atheist acknowledges the existence of evil, his argument dissolves into a moral argument for God's existence. If he denies the existence of evil, his world view is morally bankrupt. If the atheist chooses to accept the existence of evil, but not seek its ultimate cause, then atheism becomes a non-explanation of evil. Hypotheses that do not attempt to explain the data in question should be abandoned. It is not enough to say that evil is "just there."

The second difficulty with the atheistic argument from the problem of evil is the fact that, if evil exists, atheism offers absolutely no solution to the problem. After a life of suffering and pain, people die and cease to exist. I believe that the Christian solution to the problem of evil (the death, resurrection, and return of Christ) is the only hope that evil will be defeated. In fact, if Christianity is true, then Christianity guarantees the ultimate defeat of evil. The injustices of this life will be rectified in the hereafter.

CONCLUSION

In the famous debate on the existence of God between Bertrand Russell and Frederick Copleston, the atheist Bertrand Russell stated concerning the existence of the universe, "I should say that the universe is just there, and that's all."[18] It is my contention that atheism fails as an explanation of significant aspects of human experience, and that theism is a more reasonable hypothesis. If the atheist could say that "the universe is just there," could he not say that moral values, design and order, universal truths, the human experience of guilt, the sanctity of human life, the possibility of human knowledge, and meaning in life are "just there" as well. To avoid looking for an explanation is not the same thing as the search for an explanation. In this sense, the theistic explanation is superior to the atheistic explanation, for the latter reduces to a non-explanation.

However, the atheist may choose to deny the reality of moral values, design and order, universal truths, the human experience of guilt, the sanctity of human life, the possibility of human knowledge, and meaning in life. If the atheist takes this strategy, my response is that he can't live consistently with the view that these things are not real. Even the atheist lives as if some things are wrong and other things are right. He lives as if human life is sacred, and life has meaning.

Rational statements only make sense within some type of rational context. The atheist, by arguing against God's existence, has removed the rational context (the universe as an effect of the rational God) for rational discourse. He reasons against God; but if there is no God, there is no reason.

Is it reasonable to believe that the universe popped into existence out of absolute nothingness—entirely without a cause? Or, is it rational to conclude that the universe is eternal despite the strong scientific and philosophical evidences that indicate that the universe had a beginning? Is the atheist justified in holding to the idea that time plus chance plus natural laws worked upon "primordial soup" until it eventually birthed a French philosopher who declared, "I think, therefore I am"? If atheism is true, then, given enough time, it did occur. (Atheistic evolution only appears plausible in slow motion. Duane Gish stated that when we hear about a frog instantly becoming a prince, we call it a fairy tale. But if we are told that a frog became a prince gradually over a period of several million years, we call this science.)

From molecules in motion will never come moral values or the laws of logic. From a mound of dirt, a single thought will never be produced—no matter how much time is given. If no God exists and all we are is molecules in motion, from whence come human rights? If an innocent child is merely a random collection of atoms, can we really say that it is wrong to crush him? If there is no life after death and all we face is everlasting extinction, can this life really have meaning? What counsel can an atheist offer a suffering friend on his deathbed? Can we climb above despair if all we face is extinction? When the universe dies, all will die with it. If atheism is true, then human experience is a cruel joke. And, if life is a cruel joke, then why even bother to go on living?

I do not believe that we can prove God's existence with rational certainty. However, I believe that the theistic explanation is far superior to the atheistic explanation. The God of theism is an all-good God who eternally rewards those who earnestly seek Him. Either this type of God exists or He does not exist. I beseech you to choose this God, for, as the Christian thinker and scientist, Blaise Pascal, has said, if you choose God and lose, you lose nothing. But, if you choose God and He exists, you win eternity. Pascal also pointed out that if you choose against God and He does not exist, you gain nothing, but if you choose against God and He does exist, you lose everything. Therefore, the wise man will choose God.[19]

ENDNOTES

[1] Copleston, *A History of Philosophy,* vol. 2, 262-265.

[2] William Lane Craig, *Reasonable Faith* (Wheaton: Crossway Books, 1994), 91-122. J. P. Moreland, *Scaling the Secular City* (Grand Rapids: Baker Book House, 1987), 22-42.

[3] Thomas Aquinas, *Summa Theologiae,* 1a. 2,3.

[4] J. P. Moreland and Kai Nielsen, *Does God Exist? The Great Debate* (Nashville: Thomas Nelson Publishers, 1990), 35-36.

[5] Ibid., 143.

[6] Ibid., 35.

[7] Norman L. Geisler and J. Kerby Anderson, *Origin Science* (Grand Rapids: Baker Book House, 1987), 162.

[8] Ibid.

[9] Hugh Ross, *The Creator and the Cosmos* (Colorado Springs: NavPress, 1993), 111-114.

[10] Ibid., 129-132.

[11] Ibid., 127.

[12] Augustine, *On Free Will,* 2.6.

[13] C. S. Lewis, *Mere Christianity* (New York: Collier Books, 1952), 27-28.

[14] Ninian Smart, *The Religious Experience of Mankind* (New York: Charles Scribner's Sons, 1976), 40-41.

[15] Bertrand Russell, *Why I Am Not a Christian* (New York: Simon and Schuster, 1957), 107.

[16] Ibid.

[17] William Lane Craig, *No Easy Answers* (Chicago: Moody Press, 1990), 99-100.

[18] John Hick, ed., *The Existence of God,* 175.

[19] Pascal, *Pensees,* 149-155.

CHAPTER 6

OLD TESTAMENT RELIABILITY

========

Historical apologetics deals with the providing of historical evidences for the truth of Christianity. Doing historical apologetics entails several lines of argumentation. It attempts to establish the reliability of both the Old and New Testaments. It puts forth evidence for the bodily resurrection of Jesus and the deity of Christ. Finally, historical apologetics presents evidence for the Bible as God's Word.[1]

This chapter will argue that the Old Testament is a compilation of reliable historical writings. The divine authorship of the Old and New Testaments will not be argued for until chapter ten. The goal of this chapter is to show that the Old Testament is not a book of religious myths. It records historically accurate data; therefore, it should be considered historically reliable.

Since the data concerning Old Testament reliability is so extensive, this chapter will necessarily be selective. Evidence will be provided for only eight (Genesis, Exodus, Leviticus, Numbers, Deuteronomy, Joshua, Isaiah, and

Daniel) of the thirty-nine Old Testament books. However, since liberal scholars attack the reliability of these eight books more aggressively than the other Old Testament books, a strong case for the reliability of these eight books will go a long way to proving the reliability of the entire Old Testament. Most of the information in this chapter is derived from Gleason Archer's A Survey of Old Testament Introduction.[2]

THE OLD TESTAMENT MANUSCRIPTS

The Old Testament was written originally in Hebrew and Aramaic.[3] It consists of thirty-nine separate books written at different times and places between 2000BC and 400BC.[4] The three main extant Old Testament manuscripts are the Masoretic Text, the Dead Sea Scrolls, and the Septuagint.[5]

The Masoretic Text is currently considered the standard Hebrew text.[6] It dates back to about 1010AD.[7] It contains the entire Old Testament.[8] Despite its late date, it is considered the purest Hebrew text. No recent manuscript finds have brought suspicion to the Masoretic text.[9] Due to the strict copying techniques of the Masoretes, they have preserved a Hebrew text which essentially duplicates the authoritative texts of Christ's time.[10]

The Dead Sea Scrolls date back to approximately 150-100BC.[11] The Dead Sea Scrolls are the oldest extant Hebrew manuscripts of the Old Testament.[12] These scrolls were found in 1947 in various caves along the northwest coast of the Dead Sea.[13] The Dead Sea Scrolls contain fragments from every Old Testament book except Esther.[14]

The Septuagint is a Greek translation of the Hebrew Old Testament.[15] The Septuagint dates from 250-150BC.[16] When the Masoretic Text, the Dead Sea Scrolls, and the Septuagint are compared, there is essential agreement between them. The few areas of disagreement do not effect the doctrines contained in the Old Testament; the disagreements are mainly copyist errors and variations in spelling.[17]

LOWER, HIGHER, AND FORM CRITICISM

Lower criticism is the science of discovering the original text on the basis of imperfect copies.[18] This can only be done by comparing the existing copies of the passage in question. Lower criticism is essential in the task of producing accurate translations of the Old and New Testaments.

Higher criticism, on the other hand, deals with ascertaining the authorship, date, and integrity of each biblical book.[19] Higher criticism has been abused by liberal scholars who refuse to accept the evidence for the traditional Jewish and Christian view concerning the authorship, date, and integrity of the books of the Bible. This is due, in part, to the common antisupernaturalistic bias held by liberal scholars.[20] This bias rejects the possibility of revelation from God, predictive prophecies, and miracles.

Form criticism seeks to find the oral traditions that supposedly lie behind the written documents.[21] This view is highly subjective; it is often dependent upon the imagination of the scholar.

THE DOCUMENTARY HYPOTHESIS

The documentary hypothesis is the theory that the Pentateuch (the first five books of the Bible) was a compilation of different written documents composed by different authors at different places and at different times.[22] The traditional view of Moses being the author of the Pentateuch around 1450BC is rejected. The documentary hypothesis holds to much later dates for the writing of the Pentateuch.[23]

Before the eighteenth century, the Mosaic authorship of the Pentateuch was not questioned. However, the rise of deism (the belief in a non-miracle working God) led to a more skeptical approach to the Bible.[24] The process which led to the documentary hypothesis began in 1753 with the speculation of a French physician named Jean Astruc.[25] He was puzzled by the fact that God was called "Elohim" in the first chapter of Genesis, while He was primarily referred to as "Jehovah" (or Yahweh) in the second chapter.[26] He concluded that these different names for God pointed to different written sources. The sources became known as "Elohim" and "Jehovah."[27]

In the 1780's, Johann Gottfried Eichorn applied the distinction between the J (Jehovah) document and the E (Elohim) document throughout most of the Pentateuch.[28] In 1806, Wilhelm M. L. DeWette introduced the view that the entire Pentateuch was written no earlier than the reign of King David (around 1000BC).[29] DeWette also reasoned that the book of Deuteronomy (which later became known as the "D" document) was written at the start of King Josiah's reformation to unify the worship of the Jews in 621BC.[30]

In 1853, Hermann Hupfeld divided the E document into E1 and E2. The E1 document later became known as "P" (the priestly code).[31] In 1869, Abraham Kuener put the four supposed documents in what later became the standard JEDP order.[32]

In 1878, Julius Wellhausen supported this JEDP order with the evolutionary view of religion. This view teaches that man's first religion was animism (the belief that everything in nature has a life force or soul). Animism evolved into polytheism (the belief in many gods). Polytheism led to monalatry (worshiping one god as supreme over all other gods). Finally, in the evolutionary view of religion, monalatry gave rise to monotheism (the belief in one God).[33]

The gradual development of the documentary hypothesis was completed in Wellhausen's thought. According to Wellhausen, the J document was written in

850BC, while the E document was produced in 750BC. Deuteronomy was composed during King Josiah's reform in 621BC. The Priestly code was considered to be written in various stages between 570BC and 530BC.[34] This was a great departure from the traditional view which, as stated above, held that Moses was the author of all five books (around 1450BC).

REFUTATION OF THE DOCUMENTARY HYPOTHESIS

The documentary hypothesis is no longer as popular as it once was. Twentieth century scholarship has repudiated this view. Still, rather than returning to the traditional view of Mosaic authorship, twentieth century scholars have tended towards even more speculation. Several more documents have been suggested.[35]

Any evidence for the unity of the Pentateuch is explained away by asserting that a hypothetical editor supposedly put several documents together.[36] It can be said of liberal scholars that they will not allow any evidence to falsify their subjective reasoning. They speculate that two creation accounts (Genesis 1; 2) must mean two different written sources. By doing this, they reject the abundant evidence showing that ancient semitic writers often utilized a style which made use of repetition in their literature. Somehow, twentieth century liberal scholars assume they can scientifically reconstruct the text thousands of years after it was written. They even believe their speculations should hold more weight than the traditional view of the Jews who were themselves much closer to the original documents.[37]

The modern liberal scholars are guilty of circular reasoning. In their attempt to prove that the Bible is merely a human book, they assume that revelation from God is impossible.[38] In spite of the fact that much of ancient pagan history has been shown to be unreliable, liberal scholars assume that these pagan historical writings are always right when they differ from the biblical account[39] Meanwhile, again and again the Bible has been proven to be historically reliable.[40] Another weak assumption is their view that the Hebrews could use only one name for God. History reveals that ancient empires such as Babylon, Ugarit, Egypt, and Greece all had several names for their primary deity.[41] Therefore, there is no justification for speculating the existence of different authors and multiple documents merely because a different name for God (Elohim or Jehovah) is being used.

The evolutionary assumption that the Hebrew religion had evolved into monotheism is also called into question. Israel, after all, was the only nation among its ancient neighbors to have a true monotheistic faith. Israel is the exception rather than the rule. Even if one could prove that the religions of Israel's neighbors evolved towards monotheism, Israel's history is that of a nation that began with monotheism.[42]

Modern liberal scholars are notorious for taking passages out of context in order to "prove" that the Bible contains contradictions. Whenever a conservative scholar produces a possible reconciliation of the passages in question, the solution is automatically rejected by liberal scholarship.[43] Apparently, because of the common liberal bias against anything supernatural, liberal scholars will accept no argument for the traditional view of the Pentateuch.

In short, the documentary hypothesis and its updated versions do not stand on a solid foundation. They are based upon an unjustified bias against the supernatural; they also resort to fanciful speculation. The concept of the JEDP documents was created by the imaginations of liberal scholars. There is no evidence whatsoever that these documents ever existed. This is not to say that Moses did not draw upon information from written sources which predated him, but, if this was the case, objective evidence must be produced for verification. Uncontrolled subjective speculation is not true scholarship; it is the antithesis of scholarship.

EVIDENCES FOR THE MOSAIC AUTHORSHIP OF THE PENTATEUCH

Merely pointing out the inadequacies of the documentary hypothesis does not prove that Moses wrote the Pentateuch around 1450BC. Therefore, positive evidences for Mosaic authorship must be presented.

First, the entire Pentateuch displays a unity of arrangement. Even the documentarians concede this point by inventing a hypothetical editor to explain the unity of the Pentateuch.[44] This unity of arrangement strongly implies that the Pentateuch had only one author.

Second, both the Old and New Testaments call Moses the author of the Pentateuch (Joshua 8:31; 1 Kings 2:3; Daniel 9:11; Mark 12:26; Luke 20:28; John 5:46-47; 7:19; Acts 3:22; Romans 10:5). Even the Pentateuch itself declares Moses to be its author (Exodus 17:14; 24:4; 34:27; Numbers 33:1-2; Deuteronomy 31:9).[45]

Third, eyewitness details in the Pentateuch indicate the author was a participant in the events he was describing. The author at times is so precise in his details that he lists the exact number of fountains (twelve) and palm trees (seventy) in Exodus 15:27.[46] The author even describes the appearance and taste of the manna from heaven for future generations (Numbers 11:7-8).[47] These precise details make it unlikely that the author was other than an eyewitness of the events he recorded.

Fourth, the author of the Pentateuch was well acquainted with the geography and language of Egypt. He was familiar with Egyptian names and uses Egyptian figures of speech. There is a greater percentage of Egyptian words in the Pentateuch than in the rest of the Bible. This seems to indicate that the author had lived in Egypt and was most likely educated there as well. Moses was born, raised, and educated in Egypt. It is also interesting to note that the author does not attempt to explain these uniquely Egyptian factors. This probably indicates that his original readers were also familiar with the Egyptian culture, and, this is exactly the case with the Israelites that Moses led out of Egypt.[48]

Fifth, the author of the Pentateuch, although familiar with Egypt, shows himself to be unfamiliar with the land of Canaan.[49] This is consistent with Moses. After leaving Egypt, he wandered through the wilderness of Sinai, but did not enter Canaan (the promised land). The author of the Pentateuch, though he describes with great detail the geography and vegetation of Egypt and Sinai, treats the land of Canaan as a place virtually unknown to him or his people.[50] Therefore, the traditional view of Mosaic authorship is much more plausible than the documentary hypothesis.

Sixth, the setting of Exodus through Numbers is that of a desert atmosphere point of view.[51] Even the laws concerning sanitation apply to a desert lifestyle (Deuteronomy 23:12-13).[52] This would not be the case if the author or authors lived an agricultural lifestyle in their own land for nearly a thousand years (which is what the documentary hypothesis teaches).[53] Even the tabernacle (a portable tent that was the Jewish place of worship) implies a nomadic lifestyle of the worshipers.[54]

Seventh, Moses was qualified to be the author of the Pentateuch. He was educated in Egypt, grew up there, and spent much of his later life in the Sinai desert (Acts 7:22).[55]

Eighth, the customs recorded in the Pentateuch were genuine second millennium BC customs.[56] This would not be expected if the Pentateuch was written much later. This point is even stronger when it is realized that many of these customs were not continued on into the first millennium BC.

Some of these ancient customs were the legal bearing of children through maidservants, the legality of oral deathbed wills, the possessing of household idols in order to claim inheritance rights, and the way real estate transactions were practiced.[57]

Ninth, the Ras Shamra literature dates back to approximately 1400BC.[58] Therefore, writing existed during Moses' time. Hence, it cannot be argued that written languages had not developed to the degree of the Pentateuch at such an early date, which is what the documentary hypothesis teaches.

Tenth, archaeological finds have confirmed much of the history and customs reported in the Pentateuch, whereas no archaeological find has refuted the history recorded in the Bible.[59] Examples of this are the excavations of the cities of Bethel, Schechem, and Ur.[60] Archaeology has shown that these cities were inhabited as early as 2,000BC (the time of Abraham).[61] This had been denied by liberal scholars until archaeology proved them wrong and the Pentateuch right. The Hittite Legal Code, which dates back to about 1300BC, is another example. It was discovered by archaeologists between 1906 and 1912. It confirms the ancient procedure used by Abraham and several Hittites while engaging in a real estate transaction in Genesis 23.[62] Another example of archaeological confirmation of the historical reliability of the Pentateuch deals with the use of camels. Genesis records that Abraham owned camels. However, since no nonbiblical references to domesticated camels had been found, liberal scholars assumed the Pentateuch had to have been written at a much later date. However, since 1950, several archaeological findings have shown that the domestication of camels in the middle east occurred as early as 2,000BC.[63]

Eleventh, all the biblical evidence shows that the Jewish Faith was originally monotheistic, and that it later became idolatrous and polytheistic.[64] This runs counter to the evolutionary view of religion. In fact, there is no historical evidence that any nation's religion ever "evolved" into a genuine monotheistic faith. A true monotheistic faith is unique to the Jewish religion and its offshoots (Christianity, Islam, and their offshoots).[65]

Twelfth, liberal objections that the religious customs, writings, and legal code of the Jews were too advanced for the traditional fifteenth century BC date of composition have been shown to be unwarranted. Recent studies of ancient religions show that "primitive" peoples had technical sacrificial language.[66] Also, the Code of Hammurabi (1800BC) is a legal code which is very similar in its sophistication to the Law of Moses.[67] The census lists found in the ancient Semitic world (Mari, Ugarit, and Alalakh) between 2000 and 1500BC have much in common with the census lists found in the Book of Numbers.[68] Finally, Deuteronomy follows the same basic format as the Hittite suzerainty treaties (latter half of the second millennium BC), a treaty agreed upon by a king and his people.[69]

Therefore, the Pentateuch appears to be a fifteenth century BC document, and not a much later writing.

Thirteenth, ancient legends of creation and the worldwide flood are universal among primitive peoples. These legends appear to perversions of the true biblical account.[70] An example of this would be a comparison of the ancient Babylonian flood account (the Gilgames Epic) and the Genesis flood account. Whereas the boat in the Babylonian account would never float due to its dimensions, the ark's dimensions as listed in Genesis describe a vessel that would be virtually impossible to capsize.[71]

Fourteenth, the Jews accepted the Law as Mosaic during King Josiah's reform in 621BC. It is therefore hard to believe that a large portion of the Pentateuch had just been written. The Jews of that day could not have been so naive. It seems more likely that they had good reasons to believe the documents they had were copies of the ancient writings of Moses and not recent creations.[72]

Fifteenth, Moses had a good reason for using different names for the one true God. He used different names for God when dealing with different contexts. He referred to God as "Elohim" when discussing His act of creation or His infinite power. Moses seems to have called God "Jehovah" (Yahweh) when speaking of God in terms of His covenant relationship with His elect.[73] It is therefore unreasonable to assume that the utilization of various names for God requires more than one author. In fact, compound names such as Yahweh-Elohim are often used to refer to God. Yahweh-Elohim occurs eleven times in the second chapter of Genesis. It is ludicrous to assume that one compound name for God is the work of two authors writing at different times.[74]

Finally, Moses also had good reasons for varying his diction and style. Good authors commonly vary their text to prevent monotony; Moses would have done the same.[75] Moses would also have to vary his style due to the wide range of his subject material (genealogies, biographies, historical accounts, religious instruction, moral legislation, etc.).[76] The varying of the diction and style of the Pentateuch is therefore no evidence for multiple authors. Even parallel accounts (such as the two creation accounts of Genesis 1 and 2) were common by one author in ancient Semetic literature; it was often used as a type of poetic style.[77]

When all the above factors are taken together, the conclusion becomes obvious. There are extremely good reasons for accepting the traditional view that Moses wrote the Pentateuch between 1450 and 1410BC. There is absolutely no evidence for multiple authors of the Pentateuch (other than the case of Moses' obituary in Deuteronomy 34 which was probably penned by Joshua). Though Moses did apparently refer to written documents which predate him (especially while compiling Genesis), all the evidence favors the early traditional date for the Pentateuch, and not the later dates given by liberal scholars. The evidence points to Mosaic authorship. The liberal view is therefore based upon a bias against the supernatural; it is not based upon a scholarly consideration of the evidence.

JOSHUA AND THE CONQUEST OF THE PROMISED LAND

Liberal scholars of the twentieth century have denied the reliability of the biblical account of the conquest of the promised land found in the Book of Joshua. However, in 1887AD the Tell el-Amarna tablets were found. They consisted of ancient writings on clay tablets.[78] These tablets contain correspondence between Canaanite kings and the Egyptian Pharoah during a troublesome time. The Canaanite kings were requesting assistance from the Pharoah due to constant invasions by nomadic peoples called the "Habiru." Many scholars believe that the Habiru invaders, or at least many of them, were in fact the Hebrews of Joshua's army.[79] Many of the reports in the Tell el-Amarna tablets confirm specific details as related in Joshua's account of the conquest.[80]

Any descrepencies between the tablets and Joshua's account can be explained by the fact that though all Jews were Hebrews (referred to as Habiru in the tablets), not all Hebrews were Jews. For Abraham, the father of the Jewish nation, was himself a Hebrew (Genesis 14:13). Therefore, the Jews were probably not the only Hebrews invading the land of Canaan during the life of Joshua.[81]

In short, the evidence seems to indicate that there is enough agreement between the Tell el-Amarna tablets and the Book of Joshua to conclude that these tablets provide ancient secular confirmation for the Israelite conquest of the promised land (Canaan).[82] The strength of this conclusion is in no way lessened by the fact that the Habiru invaders of the tablets cannot in every case be equated with Joshua's army.

THE BOOK OF ISAIAH

Liberal scholars have rejected the traditional view that Isaiah wrote the Book of Isaiah between 740 and 680BC. In an attempt to explain away the supernatural ful-fillment of predictive prophecies, these scholars have con-cluded that there were actually two authors who wrote Isaiah. This is called the "Deutero-Isaiah Theory."[83] They argue that one author wrote the first thirty-nine chapters, while a different author wrote the last twenty-seven chap-ters.[84] The second author is assumed to have lived in Babylon after the Babylonian Empire had taken the Jews captive in 586BC. If the book is merely a human book (as liberal scholars claim), then, since the last twenty-seven chapters speak of the Babylonian captivity, it must be dated after that event occurred.

Several things can be noted to refute the Deutero-Isaiah theory. First, the entire book of Isaiah exhibits a sim-ilar writing style. In fact, conservative scholars have located over forty sentences or phrases that exist in both halves of Isaiah.[85] One would not expect this if there were more than one author. Second, the author is familiar with the Palestine area; he is not familiar with Babylon.[86] However, if the sec-ond half of Isaiah was written by a Jew living in Babylon, this would not be the case. Third, Jesus apparently believed that Isaiah wrote both halves of the Book of Isaiah. In one New Testament passage, He quoted from both Isaiah 53 and Isaiah 6 and referred to Isaiah as the author of both (John 12:37-41).[87] Fourth, a prediction of the Medo-Persian over-throw of the Babylonian Empire is mentioned in the first half of Isaiah (Isaiah 13:17-19). This Medo-Persian con-quest occurred in 538BC. Even liberal scholars admit that this section of Isaiah was written before the Babylonian captivity (586BC).[88] If the author could predict the future in the first thirty-nine chapters, he could certainly do the same in the last twenty-seven chapters.

There is no good reason to reject the traditional date and authorship of Isaiah; only a bias against the supernatural will cause a scholar to reject the traditional view despite the evidence in its favor. Isaiah chapter 53 is a case in point. It is probably Isaiah's most famous prophecy. In this chapter, Isaiah predicts that the Jewish Messiah would suffer for the iniquities of His people. Since this did not occur until 30AD, there is no way for scholars to date any portion of the Book of Isaiah this late.[89] Therefore, no matter how late Isaiah is dated, the fulfillment of predictive proheies must be admitted. Hence, the liberal bias against the supernatural is without justification.

THE BOOK OF DANIEL

Thr traditional view concerning the Book of Daniel is that Daniel wrote it between 590 and 530BC.[90] Daniel lived under both the Babylonian and the Medo-Persian rule over Judah.

The liberal view teaches that the Book of Daniel was written around 165BC to encourage the Jews in Palestine to resist the evil ruler Antiochus Epiphanes.[91] This is due to the fact that Daniel predicts the reign of this vile man. And, as mentioned throughout this chapter, liberal scholars reject the fulfillment of predictive prophecies. Their world view forces them to date the Book of Daniel after the events occurred. Hence, they assume the late date.[92]

There is much evidence for the traditional date of Daniel. First, Daniel uses early Aramaic which is consistent with the sixth century BC date of composition, rather than a second century BC date.[93] Second, the three Greek words found in Daniel do not prove a late date (the Greeks did not takeover the Palestine area until 330BC). The three Greek words are names of musical instruments, which could easily have been known and used in Palestine and Babylon long before the Greeks conquered those regions.[94]

Third, Daniel's theology, contrary to liberal speculation, was not too advanced for such an early date as the sixth century BC. His teaching concerning angels, the end-time resurrection, and the Kingdom of God can also be found in other Old Testament books which predate the sixth century BC.[95]

Fourth, there is strong archaeological confirmation of some of the historical characters found in the Book of Daniel. King Belshazzar was thought to be unhistorical by liberal critics. Secular history records Nabonidus as the last king of the Babylonian Empire. However, later discoveries of cuneiform tablets revealed that Nabonidus shared his reign with his son Belshazzar.[96] Liberal scholars also rejected the historicity of Darius the Mede, but recent scholarship has identified Darius the Mede with an ancient govenor of Babylon named Gubaru. It has also been shown that Darius was probably not a personal name; rather, it was a title of royalty (such as Caesar was for the Romans).[97]

Fifth, several of Daniel's predictions were fulfilled after 165BC.[98] Therefore, there is no reason to date the Book of Daniel around that time. Daniel's prophecies of the four world kingdoms (Daniel 2, 7) predicted that the Medo-Persians would overthrow the Babylonians (this occurred in 538BC). Daniel foretold the Greek conquest of the Medo-Persian Empire (330BC). But, Daniel also prophesied the Roman conquest of Palestine, which occurred in 63BC. This is obviously much later than even the most liberal dating of Daniel (165BC). Hence, there is no way to avoid the conclusion that Daniel contains predictive prophecies that have been fulfilled.[99]

Some of Daniel's most amazing prophecies are

Messianic. Daniel predicted that the Messiah would be executed 483 years after the order to rebuild the walls of
Jerusalem was issued (Daniel 9:24-27). This would place
the death of the Jewish Messiah at about 30AD.[100] Daniel
also stated that the death of the Messiah would be followed
by the destruction of the temple in Jerusalem (which
occurred in 70AD).[101]

No matter how one tries, there is no way to remove
the supernatural elements from the Book of Daniel. Even if
a person accepts the liberal dating of the book of Daniel
(165BC), it is still evident that Daniel predicted the future.
He predicted future events that did not occur until after
165BC. Therefore, there is no reason to attempt to date
Daniel after the events he predicts, for even the late date for
the composition of Daniel must admit the fulfillment of
predictive prophecies. Since even the liberal 165BC date
would have to admit major fulfillments of prophecies, the
evidence supports the traditional date (590-530BC) for the
Book of Daniel.

CONCLUSION

The Old Testament has been shown to be historically
reliable. Many times archaeology has confirmed the Old testament account. Not once has an archaeological find refuted
the history recorded in the Bible.[102] The only reason to
reject the historical reliability of the Old Testament is an a
priori bias against the possibility of God revealing Himself
through propositional form, and, as has been shown, this
bias is unwarranted.

ENDNOTES

[1] Geisler, *Apologetics*, 285-377.

[2] Gleason L. Archer, Jr., *A Survey of Old Testament Introduction* (Chicago:

Moody Press, 1974), entire book.

[3] Ibid., 15.

[4] Ibid., 19.

[5] Ibid., 37-45.

[6] Ibid., 44.

[7] Ibid.

[8] Ibid.

[9] Ibid., 42.

[10] Ibid., 66.

[11] Ibid., 38.

[12] Josh McDowell, *Evidence That Demands a Verdict* (Here's Life Publishers, 1974), 57-58.

[13] Archer, 37.

[14] Merrill C. Tenney, ed., *The Zondervan Pictorial Bible Dictionary,* (Grand Rapids: Zondervan Pub;lishing House, 1967), 206.

[15] Archer, 45.

[16] Ibid.

[17] McDowell, Evidence, 58.

[18] Archer, 55.

[19] Ibid.

[20] Ibid., 109-110.

[21] Ibid., 97-98.

[22] Ibid., 83-84.

[23] Ibid.

[24] Ibid., 83.

[25] Ibid., 84.

[26] Ibid.

[27] Ibid.

[28] Ibid.

[29] Ibid.

[30] Ibid., 85.

[31] Ibid., 87-88.

[32] Ibid., 89.

[33] Ibid., 89-90, 148-150.

[34] Ibid., 91-92.

[35] Ibid., 94.

[36] Ibid., 110.

[37] Ibid., 112.

[38] Ibid., 109.

[39] Ibid., 110-111.

[40] Ibid., 111.

[41] Ibid., 110.

[42] Ibid., 111.

[43] Ibid., 111-112.

[44] Ibid., 121-122.

[45] Ibid., 113-114.

[46] Ibid., 115.

[47] Ibid.

[48] Ibid., 115-119.

[49] Ibid., 119-120.

[50] Ibid.

[51] Ibid., 120.

[52] Ibid.

[53] Ibid.

[54] Ibid.

[55] Ibid., 114-115, 122-123.

[56] Ibid., 120.

[57] Ibid., 164.

[58] Ibid., 170, 172.

[59] Ibid., 170-182.

[60] Ibid., 173-174.

[61] Ibid.

[62] Ibid., 176-177.

[63] Ibid., 177.

[64] Ibid., 147-169.

[65] Ibid., 149.

[66] Ibid., 179.

[67] Ibid., 177.

[68] Charles F. Pfeiffer and Everett F. Harrison, eds., *The Wycliffe Bible Commentary* (Nashville: The Southwestern Company, 1962), 115.

[69] Archer, 259-260.

[70] John J. Davis, *Paradise to Prison* (Grand Rapids: Baker Book House, 1975), 129-133.

[71] Henry M. Morris, *The Genesis Record* (Grand Rapids: Baker Book House, 1976), 181.

[72] Archer, 259-268.

[73] Ibid., 124-129.

[74] Ibid., 126.

[75] Ibid., 130.

[76] Ibid., 129.

[77] Ibid., 132-135, 138.

[78] Ibid., 271.

[79] Ibid., 276.

[80] Ibid.

[81] Ibid., 277.

[82] Ibid.

[83] Ibid., 336-338.

[84] Ibid.

[85] Ibid., 352.

[86] Ibid., 357.

[87] Ibid., 356.

[88] Ibid., 357.

[89] Ibid., 355.

[90] Ibid., 387.

[91] Ibid., 388.

[92] Ibid.

[93] Ibid., 398-401.

[94] Ibid., 395.

[95] Ibid., 403.

[96] Ibid., 390-392.

[97] Ibid., 393-394.

[98] Ibid., 403-408.

[99] Ibid., 407.

[100] Ibid., 409.

[101] Ibid.

[102] Ibid., 171.

CHAPTER 7

NEW TESTAMENT RELIABILITY

E stablishing the reliability of the New Testament is vital to Christian apologetics. Christianity is a religion with deep historical roots. For example, if Jesus did not rise from the dead (an historical event), then the Christian Faith cannot save (1 Corinthians 15:14, 17). If He did not die on the cross for the sins of mankind (an historical event), then Christianity offers no hope (1 Peter 2:24; 3:18). Proving the New Testament can be trusted will go a long way to establishing Christianity as the one true faith.

This chapter will attempt to show that the New Testament accounts were written by eyewitnesses who knew Christ, or persons who knew the eyewitnesses. Evidence will be provided to show that the accounts of Christ's bodily resurrection and His claims to deity were not legends invented decades after Christ's death; rather, they were eyewitness accounts. This chapter will not deal with defending the Bible as the inspired and inerrant Word of God; that topic will be examined in chapter ten. The purpose of this chapter is to merely show that the New Testament documents are historically reliable.

MANUSCRIPT EVIDENCE OF THE NEW TESTAMENT

Many historical scholars believe that one cannot know the true Jesus of history since no one no has the original writings of those who knew Him. Only copies of the originals are in existence today. Ironically, these historical scholars will often quote from Plato, as well as other ancient writers, as if they can know with certainty what Plato originally wrote. This clearly unveils a double standard. Ancient secular writings can be trusted based on late copies, but the New Testament cannot be trusted since the original manuscripts are missing.

The New Testament is by far the most reliable ancient writing in existence today. There exist today over 24,000 copies (5,000 of them in the original Greek language) of the New Testament (either in whole or in part).[1] This should be compared with the fact that only 7 copies presently exist of Plato's Tetralogies.[2] Homer's Iliad is in second place behind the New Testament among ancient writings with just 643 copies.[3]

The earliest copy of Plato's Tetralogies is dated about 1,200 years after Plato supposedly wrote the original.[4] Compare this with the earliest extant copy of the New Testament: the John Ryland's Papyri. It contains a portion of John 18. This fragment is dated at about 125AD, only 25 years after the original is thought to have been written.[5] In fact, there is possibly an even earlier New Testament fragment that was found among the Dead Sea Scrolls. The fragment is called 7Q5; it is dated earlier than 70AD. Though there is heated debate about this manuscript, it has been argued that it is a part of Mark 6:52-53.[6] Again, Homer's Iliad takes second place among ancient writings, second only to the New Testament. The earliest copy of any portion of Homer's Iliad is dated about 500 years after the original writing.[7]

When the contents of the extant manuscripts of the New Testament are compared, there appears to be 99.5% agreement. There is total agreement in the doctrines taught; the corruptions are mainly grammatical.[8] Homer's Iliad once again takes second place behind the New Testament among ancient documents. Homer's Iliad has a 95% accuracy when its copies are compared.[9] Since there are so few remaining copies of Plator's writings, agreement between these copies is not considered a factor (they are probably all copies of the same copy).[10]

TABLE 1

COMPARISON OF 3 ANCIENT WRITINGS

Ancient Writing Between Copies	Extant Copies	Earliest Extant Copy	Agreement
Homer's Iliad	643	500 years after original	95%
Plato's Tetralogies	7	1,200 years after original	—
New Testament	24,000	25 years after original	99.5%

In short, historical scholars can consider the extant New Testament manuscripts to be reliable and accurate representations of what the authors originally wrote. Since the New Testament is by far the most accurately copied ancient writing, to question its authenticity is to call into question all of ancient literature.

ANCIENT NEW TESTAMENT COPIES

The following manuscripts are some of the better known copies of the New Testament. The John Rylands Papyri is the oldest undisputed fragment of the New Testament still in existence. It is dated between 125 and 130AD. It contains a portion of John 18.[11] The Bodmer Papyrus II contains most of John's Gospel and dates between 150 and 200AD.[12] The Chester Beatty Papyri includes major portions of the New Testament; it is dated around 200AD.[13]

Codex Vaticanus contains nearly the entire Bible and is dated between 325 and 350AD.[14] Codex Sinaiticus contains nearly all of the New Testament and approximately half of the Old Testament. It is dated at about 350AD.[15] Codex Alexandrinus encompasses almost the entire Bible and was copied around 400AD.[16] Codex Ephraemi represents every New Testament book except for 2 John and 2 Thessalonians. Ephraemi is dated in the 400's AD.[17] Codex Bezae has the Gospels and Acts as its contents and is dated after 450AD.[18]

TABLE 2

ANCIENT NEW TESTAMENT COPIES

Manuscript	Contents	Date
John Rylands Papyri	portion of John 18	125-130AD
Bodmer Papyrus II	most of John's Gospel	150-200AD
Chester Beatty Papyri	major portions. of N. T.	200AD

Codex Vaticanus	almost entire Bible	325-350AD
Codex Sinaiticus	all of N. T. & half of O. T.	350AD
Codex Alexandrinus	almost entire Bible	400AD
Codex Ephraemi	most of N. T.	400's AD
Codex Bezae	the Gospels & Acts	450AD

The very early dates of these manuscripts provide strong evidence that the content of the current New Testament is one and the same with the original writings of the apostles. There is no logical reason to doubt the reliability of these manuscripts.

THE APOSTOLIC FATHERS: ANOTHER SOURCE OF N. T. RELABILITY

The New Testament manuscripts are not the only evidence for the reliability of the New Testament. Another source of evidence is found in the writings of the apostolic fathers. The apostolic fathers were leaders in the early church who knew the apostles and their doctrine.[19] Most of their writings were produced between 95 and 150AD.[20]

Liberal scholars have attempted to find the so-called true Jesus of history. It was their goal to find a non-supernatural Jesus who never claimed to be God. These scholars believe that Christ's claim to be God and Savior, and His miraculous life (especially His bodily resurrection from the dead) are merely legends. The true Jesus of history was a great teacher; still, He was merely a man.[21] Therefore, if it can be shown that early church leaders, who personally knew the apostles, taught that the miraculous aspects of Christ's life actually occurred and that Jesus did in fact make the bold claims recorded in the New Testament, then the legend hypothesis fails. Historians recognize that legends take centuries to develop.[22] A legend is a ficticious story that, through the passage of time, many people come to accept as historically accurate. A legend can begin to develop only if the eyewitnesses and those who knew the eyewitnesses are already dead. Otherwise, the eyewitnesses or those who knew them would refute the legend. Therefore, a legend has its beginning a generation or two after the event or person in question has passed. However, before a legend receives wide acceptance, several centuries are needed, for there is still a remembrance of the person or event due to information passed on orally from generation to generation. After several centuries, new generations arise without the sufficient knowledge of the person or event necessary to refute the legend. If a written record compiled by eyewitnesses is passed on to future generations, legends can be easily refuted.

One apostolic father, Clement, was the Bishop of Rome. He wrote his letter to the Corinthians in 95AD. The following is a brief quote from this letter:

> Let us fear the Lord Jesus (Christ), whose blood was given for us.[23] The Apostles received the Gospel for us from the Lord Jesus Christ; Jesus Christ was sent from God.[24] He made the Lord Jesus Christ the firstfruit, when He raised Him from the dead.[25]

It is important to note that Clement of Rome referred to Jesus as "the Lord." This is an obvious reference to Christ's deity, for he uses the Greek word "Kurios" with the definite article[26] (Christ was the Lord, not a Lord). Clement also spoke of Christ's blood as being shed for us, indicating a belief in Christ's saving work. He declared that the apostles received the Gospel directly from Jesus. Clement also spoke of God raising Jesus from the dead. If any of these statements were opposed to the doctrines of the apostles, the Apostle John, who was still alive at the time, would have openly confronted this first century bishop. However, he did not. Therefore, the writings of Clement of Rome provide strong confirmation of the original message of the Apostles. Contrary to the wishful thinking of skeptics, the teachings of the first century church are exactly what one finds in the New Testament.

The apostolic father, Ignatius, bishop of Antioch, wrote his letters between 110 and 115AD. During that time, he was travelling from Antioch to Rome to be martyred.[27] Ignatius openly wrote about the deity of Christ. He referred to Jesus as "Jesus Christ our God," "God in man," and "Jesus Christ the God."[28] Ignatius stated that "there is one God who manifested Himself through Jesus Christ His Son."[29] Besides ascribing deity to Christ, Ignatius also wrote of salvation in Christ and expressed belief in Christ's virgin birth, crucifixion, and resurrection:

> Christ Jesus our Savior . . .[30]
>
> Jesus Christ, who dies for us, that believing on His death ye might escape death.[31]
>
> He is truly of the race of David according to the flesh, but Son of God by the Divine will and power, truly born of a virgin.[32]
>
> Be ye deaf therefore, when any man speaketh to you apart from Jesus Christ, who was born of the race of David, who was the Son of Mary, who was truly born and ate and drank, was truly persecuted under Pontius Pilate, was truly crucified and died in the sight of those in heaven and those on earth and those under the earth; who moreover was truly raised from the dead, His Father having raised Him . . .[33]

The writings of Ignatius show that only fifteen years after the death of the Apostle John, the central doctrines of the New Testament were already being taught. It is highly unlikely that the New Testament manuscripts, referenced by Ignatius, could have been corrupted in such a short amount of time. It is also important to remember that Clement of Rome taught the same doctrines while the Apostle John was still alive.

Another apostolic father Polycarp (70-156AD) was the Bishop of Smyrna. He was a personal pupil of the Apostle John.[34] Had any of the other apostolic fathers perverted the teachings of the apostles, Polycarp would have set the record straight. However, Polycarp's teachings are essentially the same as that of Clement of Rome and Ignatius. Of all the apostolic fathers, Polycarp knew better than any the content of the original apostles' message. Liberal scholars display tremendous arrogance when thay assume that they have more insight into the original apostolic message than Polycarp. Polycarp studied under the Apostle John (85-95AD?); contemporary scholars live nearly 2,000 years later. In his letter to the Philippians, Polycarp wrote:

> . . . Jesus Christ who took our sins in His own body upon the tree, who did no sin, neither was guile found in His mouth, but for our sakes He endured all things, that we might live in Him.[35]
>
> For they loved not the present world, but Him that died for our sakes and was raised by God for us.[36]
>
> . . . who shall believe on our Lord and God Jesus Christ and on His Father that raised Him from the dead.[37]

Another student of the Apostle John was Papias, the Bishop of Hierapolis. Papias was born between 60 and 70AD and died between 130 and 140AD.[38] Papias wrote that he did not accept the words of any self-proclaimed teacher. Instead, he would talk to others who, like himself, had known at least one of the original apostles. In this way, Papias could discover the teachings of Christ from the sources closest to Christ Himself, rather than rely on hearsay testimony.[39]

Papias wrote of his discussions with persons who spoke with with apostles such as Andrew, Peter, Philip, Thomas, James, John, or Matthew.[40] Papias stated that Mark received the information for his Gospel from the Apostle Peter himself. Papias also related that Matthew originally recorded his gospel in Hebrew, but that it was later translated into Greek to reach a wider audience.[41]

The testimony of the first century and early second century church should be considered extremely reliable. Many of these early Christians were martyred for their beliefs. Since people will only die for what they truly believe, it is reasonable to conclude that the early church sincerely believed thay were protecting the true apostolic faith from possible perversions. If they had tampered with the teachings of the apostles, they certainly would not have died for their counterfeit views.

The following conclusions can now be drawn: First, the apostolic fathers form an unbroken chain from the apostles to their day. Second, people who personally knew the apostles accepted the leadership of the apostolic fathers. Third, the apostolic fathers taught essentially the same thing as the New Testament. Fourth, the apostolic fathers and their followers were willing to die for the teachings passed down to them from the apostles themselves. Therefore, our New Testament accurately represents the teachings of the apostles. This includes such key doctrines as the deity of Christ,

His substitutionary death, virgin birth, bodily resurrection, and salvation through Him alone.

ANCIENT SECULAR WRITINGS: ANOTHER WITNESS

Besides references to Christ in Christian literature which dates back to the first and second centuries AD, there are also ancient secular writings which refer to Christ from that same time period. The significance of these non-Christian writings is that, though the secular authors themselves did not believe the early church's message, they stated the content of what the early church actually taught.

In 52AD, Thallus recorded a history of the Eastern Mediterranean world. In this work, he covered the time period from the Trojan War (mid 1200's BC) to his day (52AD). Though no manuscripts of Thallus' work are known to currently exist, Julius Africanus (writing in 221AD) referred to Thallus' work. Africanus stated that Thallus attempted to explain away the darkness that covered the land when Christ was crucified. Thallus attributed this darkness to an eclipse of the sun.[42] This reveals that about twenty years after the death of Christ, non-believers were still trying to give explanations for the miraculous events of Christ's life.

In 115AD, a Roman historian named Cornelius Tacitus wrote about the great fire of Rome which occurred during Nero's reign. Tacitus reported that Nero blamed the fire on a group of people called Christians, and he tortured them for it. Tacitus stated that the Christians had been named after their founder "Christus." Tacitus said that Christus had been executed by Pontius Pilate during the reign of Tiberius (14-37AD). Tacitus related that the "superstition" of the Christians had been stopped for a short time, but then once again broke out, spreading from Judaea all the way to Rome. He said that multitudes of Christians (based on their own confessions to be followers of Christ) were thrown to wild dogs, crucified, or burned to death. Tacitus added that their persecutions were not really for the good of the public; their deaths merely satisfied the cruelty of Nero himself.[43]

These statements by Tacitus are consistent with the New Testament records. Even Tacitus' report of the stopping of the "superstition" and then its breaking out again appears to be his attempt to explain how the death of Christ stifled the spreading of the gospel, but then the Christian message was once again preached, this time spreading more rapidly. This is perfectly consistent with the New Testament record. The New Testament reports that Christ's disciples went into hiding during His arrest and death. After Jesus rose from the dead (three days after the crucifixion), He filled His disciples with the Holy Spirit (about fifty days after the crucifixion), and they fearlessly proclaimed the gospel throughout the Roman Empire (Acts 1 and 2).

Suetonius was the chief secretary of Emperor Hadrian who reigned over Rome from 117 to 138AD. Suetonius refers to the riots that occurred in the Jewish community in Rome in 49AD due to the instigation of "Chrestus." Chrestus is apparently a variant spelling of Christ. Suetonius refers to these Jews being expelled from the city.[44] Seutonius also reports that following the great fire of Rome, Christians were punished. He refers to their religious beliefs as "new and mischievous."[45]

Pliny the Younger, another ancient secular writer, provides evidence for early Christianity. He was a Roman govenor in Asia Minor. His work dates back to 112AD. He states that Christians assembled on a set day, sangs hymns to Christ as to a god, vowed not to partake in wicked deeds, and shared "ordinary" food.[46] This shows that by 112AD, it was already common knowledge that Christians worshipped Christ, sang hymns to Him, lived moral lives, assembled regularly, and partook of common food (probably a reference to the celebration of the Lord's Supper).

The Roman Emperor Trajan also wrote in 112AD. He gave guidelines for the persecution of Christians. He stated that if a person denies he is a Christian and proves it by worshiping the Roman gods, he must be pardoned for his repentance.[47]

The Roman Emperor Hadrian reigned from 117 to 138AD. He wrote that Christians should only be punished if there was clear evidence against them. Mere accusations were not enough to condemn a supposed Christian.[48] The significance of these passages found in the writings of Trajan and Hadrian is that it confirms the fact that early Christians were sincere enough about their beliefs to die for them.

The Talmud is the written form of the oral traditions of the ancient Jewish Rabbis. A Talmud passage dating back to between 70 and 200AD refers to Jesus as one who "practised sorcery" and led Israel astray. This passage states that Jesus (spelled Yeshu) was hanged (the common Jewish term for crucifixion) on the night before the Passover feast.[49] This is a very significant passage, for it reveals that even the enemies of Christ admitted there were supernatural aspects of Christ's life by desribing Him as one who "practiced sorcery." This source also confirms that Jesus was crucified around the time of the Passover feast.

Another anti-Christian document was the Toledoth Jesu, which dates back to the fifth century AD, but reflects a much earlier Jewish tradition. In this document, the Jewish leaders are said to have paraded the rotting corpse of Christ through the streets of Jerusalem.[50] This obviously did not occur. The earliest preaching of the gospel took place in Jerusalem. Therefore, parading the rotting corpse of Christ through the streets of Jerusalem would have crushed the Christian faith in its embryonic stage. However, some of the other non-Christian authors mentioned above stated that Christianity spread rapidly during the first few decades after Christ's death. The preaching of Christ's resurrection would not have been persuasive if His rotting corpse had been publicly displayed.

It is also interesting to note that the Jewish religious leaders waited quite a long before putting a refutation of the resurrection into print. Certainly, it would have served their best interests to disprove Christ's resurrection. But as far as written documents are concerned, the first century Jewish authorities were silent regarding the resurrection of Jesus.

Lucian was a Greek satirist of the second century. He wrote that Christians worshiped a wise man who had been crucified, lived by His laws, and believed themselves to be immortal.[51] Thus, this ancient secular source confirms the New Testament message by reporting the fact that Jesus was worshiped by His earliest followers.

Probably the most interesting of all ancient non-Christian references to the life of Christ is found in the writings of the Jewish historian named Joephus. Joephus was born in 37 or 38AD and died in 97AD. At nineteen, he became a Pharisee (a Jewish religious leader and teacher).[52] The following passage is found in his writings:

> Now there was about this time Jesus, a wise man, if it be lawful to call him a man; for he was a doer of wonderful works, a teacher of such men as receive the truth with pleasure. He drew over to him both many of the Jews and many of the Gentiles. He was (the) Christ. And when Pilate, at the suggestion of the principal men amongst us, had condemned him to the cross, those that loved him at the first did not forsake him; for he appeared to them alive again the third day; as the divine prophets had foretold these and ten thousand other

wonderful things concerning him. And the tribe of Christians, so named after him, are not extinct at this day.[53]

Since Josephus was a Jew and not a Christian, many scholars deny that this passage was originally written by him. These scholars believe this text was corrupted by Christians. Gary Habermas, chairman of the the philosophy department at Liberty University, dealt with this problem in the following manner:

There are good indications that the majority of the text is genuine. There is no textual evidence against it, and, conversely, there is very good manuscript evidence for this statement about Jesus, thus making it difficult to ignore. Additionally, leading scholars on the works of Josephus have testified that this portion is written in the style of this Jewish historian. Thus we conclude that there are good reasons for accepting this version of Josephus' statement about Jesus, with modifications of questionable words. In fact, it is possible that these modifications can even be accurately ascertained. In 1972 Professor Schlomo Pines of the Hebrew University in Jerusalem released the results of a study on an Arabic manuscript containing Josephus' statement about Jesus. It includes a different and briefer rendering of the entire passage, including changes in the key words listed above. . .[54]

Habermas goes on to relate the Arabic version of this debated passage. In this version, Jesus is described as being a wise and virtuous man who had many followers from different nations. He was crucified under Pontius Pilate, but his disciples reported that, three days later, He appeared to them alive. Josephus added that Jesus may have been the Messiah whom the prophets had predicted would come.[55]

It is highly unlikely that both readings of this controversial passage are corrupt. One of these two readings probably represents the original text. The other reading would then be a copy that was tampered with by either a Christian or a non-Christian. Whatever the case may be, even the skeptic should have no problem accepting the Arabic reading. Still, even if only this reading is accepted, it is enough. For it is a first century testimony from a non-Christian historian that declares that those who knew Jesus personally claimed that He had appeared to them alive three days after His death by crucifixion under Pilate.

Several things can be learned from this brief survey of ancient non-Christian writings concerning the life of Christ. First, His earliest followers worshiped Him as God. The doctrine of Christ's deity is therefore not a legend or myth developed many years after Christ's death (as was the case with Buddha). Second, they claimed to have seen Him alive three days after His death. Third, Christ's earliest followers faced persecution and martyrdom for their refusal to deny His deity and resurrection. Therefore, the deity and resurrection of Christ were not legends added to the text centuries after its original composition. Instead, these teachings were the focus of the teaching of Christ's earliest followers. They claimed to be eyewitnesses of Christ's miraculous life and were willing to die horrible deaths for their testimonies. Therefore, they were reliable witnesses of who the true Jesus of history was and what He taught.

ANCIENT CREEDS FOUND IN THE NEW TESTAMENT

The writings of both the apostolic fathers and ancient non-Christian authors declare that the earliest

Christians did in fact teach that Jesus is God and that He rose from the dead. The manuscript evidence for the New Testament is stronger than that of any other ancient writing. Another piece of evidence for the authenticity and reliability of the New Testament manuscripts is the ancient creeds found in the New Testament itself.

Most scholars, whether liberal or conservative, date Paul's epistles before the Gospels were put into written form.[56] Just as the teachings of the Jewish Rabbis had originally been passed on orally, it appears that the Gospel was first spread in the form of oral creeds and hymns.[57] J. P. Moreland states that Paul's epistles contain many of these pre-Pauline creeds and hymns, that they were originally spoken in the Aramaic tongue (the Hebrew language of Christ's day), and that most scholars date these creeds and hymns between 33AD and 48AD.[58] Since Paul's writings are dated in the 50's AD or 60's AD by most scholars, the creeds he recorded in his letters point to an oral tradition which predates his writings. Most scholars will at least admit that these ancient creeds originated before 50AD.[59]

Excerpts from some of these ancient creeds found in the letters of Paul are as follows:

. . . that if you confess with your mouth Jesus as Lord, and believe in your heart that God raised Him from the dead, you shall be saved (Romans 10:9).

For I delivered to you as of first importance what I also received, that Christ died for our sins according to the Scriptures, and that He was buried, and that He was raised on the third day according to the Scriptures, and that He appeared to Cephas, then to the twelve. After that He appeared to more than five hundred brethren at one time, most of whom remain until now, but some have fallen asleep; then He appeared to James, then to all the apostles; and last of all, as it were to one untimely born, He appeared to me also (1 Corinthians 15:3-8).

Have this attitude in yourselves which was also in Christ Jesus, who, although He existed in the form of God, did not regard equality with God a thing to be grasped, but emptied Himself, taking the form of a bondservant, and being made in the likeness of men. And being found in appearance as a man, He humbled Himself by becoming obedient to the point of death, even death on a cross. Therefore also God highly exalted Him, and bestowed on Him the name which is above every name, that at the name of Jesus every knee should bow, of those who are in heaven, and on earth, and under the earth, and that every tongue should confess that Jesus Christ is Lord, to the glory of God the Father (Philippians 2:5-11).

And He [Christ] is the image of the invisible God, the first-born of all creation. For by Him all things were created, both in the heavens and on earth, visible and invisible, whether thrones or dominions or rulers or authorities—all things have been created by Him and for Him. And He is before all things, and in Him all things hold together (Colossians 1:15-17).

These ancient creeds clearly prove that the first generation Christians believed that Jesus had risen bodily from the dead, that He is God, and that salvation comes through Him.[60] The followers of Buddha attributed deity to the founder of their religion centuries after his death.[61] However, the earliest followers of Christ, those who knew Him personally, considered Him to be God.[62] It is almost universally recognized that these creeds were formulated before 50AD. Therefore, they represent the Gospel in its original form.

The belief in Christ's deity and resurrection is not based on later corruptions of the New Testament text as liberal scholars believe. The doctrines of Christ's deity and resurrection are not legends that took centuries to develop. These doctrines were held by the first generation church, those who knew Jesus personally. The gospel message found in the New Testament is the same message proclaimed by the apostles themselves.

Less than twenty years after Christ's death, hymns were already being sung in Christian churches attributing deity to Christ. The apostles were still alive and had the authority to supress the doctrine of Christ's deity if it was a heresy, but, they did not. All the available evidence indicates that they not only condoned it, but that it was their own teaching. Therefore, liberal scholars such as John Hick have no justification for their claims that the deity of Christ was a legend that developed near the end of the first century AD.[63] The historical evidence indicates that the Christian church always believed in Christ's deity. Therefore, to deny that Christ claimed to be God is to call the apostles liars.

Nearly 2,000 years after the death of Christ a forum of liberal scholars called the "Jesus Seminar" has been meeting since 1985. These scholars vote to decide which biblical passages they believe Jesus actually said.[64] This is ironic since the evidence shows that Christianity proclaimed Christ's deity and resurrection from its inception. The early church accepted the deity of Christ. The early church was willing to suffer horrible persecution for this belief. Sincere eyewitness testimony should not be ignored.

THE OPINIONS OF THE EXPERTS

The testimonies of some of the world's leading experts can be called upon to further verify the authenticity and reliability of the New Testament manuscripts. Dr. John A. T. Robinson, one of England's leading New Testament critics, came to the conclusion that the entire New Testament was written before the fall of Jerusalem in 70AD.[65]

Sir William Ramsey was one of the world's greatest archaeologists. His thorough investigation into Luke's Book of Acts led him to the conclusion that Acts was a mid-first century document that was historically reliable.[66]

William F. Albright is one of the world's foremost biblical archaeologists. He states that there is no evidential basis for dating any New Testament book after 80AD.[67]

Sir Frederic Kenyon was one of the world's leading experts on ancient manuscripts. His research led him to conclude that the New Testament is essentially the same as when it was originally written.[68]

Millar Burrows, the great archaeologist from Yale, stated that there is no doubt that archaeological research has strengthened confidence in the historical reliability of the Bible. Burrows also stated that the skepticism of liberal scholars is based on their prejudice against the supernatural, rather than on the evidence itself.[69]

F. F. Bruce, New Testament scholar from Manchester University in England, stated that if the New Testament writings had been secular works, no scholar would question their authenticity. Bruce believes that the evidence for the New Testament outweighs the evidence for many classical works which have never been doubted.[70]

Bruce Metzger is a famous textual critic from Princeton. He has stated that the New Testament has more evidence in its favor than any other writings from ancient Greek or Latin literature.[71]

It is clear that the evidence favors the authenticity and reliability of the New Testament. Scholars who do not allow their bias against the supernatural to influence their conclusions have recognized this fact. Scholars who reject the reliability of the New Testament manuscripts do so because they chose to go against the overwhelming evidence. However, such a rejection is not true scholarship; it is an a priori assumption.

CONCLUSION

Evidence from the existing New Testament manuscripts, from the writings of the apostolic fathers, from the works of ancient secular authors, from the ancient creeds and hymns found in the New Testament, and from the opinions of the world's leading experts have been examined. All this evidence leads to the conclusion that the existing New Testament manuscripts are reliable and authentic testimony of what the apostles wrote. A person is free to deny this conclusion, but to do so is to go against all the available evidence.

The key point is that the original apostles taught that Jesus rose from the dead, and that He claimed to be God incarnate and the Savior of the world.

ENDNOTES

[1] McDowell, *Evidence,* 42-43.

[2] Ibid.

[3] Ibid., 43.

[4] Ibid.

[5] Ibid.

[6] Winfried Corduan, *Reasonable Faith* (Nashville: Broadman and Holman Publishers, 1993), 192.

[7] McDowell, *Evidence,* 43.

[8] Ibid.

[9] Ibid.

[10] Ibid.

[11] Ibid., 46.

[12] Ibid., 46-47.

[13] Ibid., 47.

[14] Ibid.

[15] Ibid., 47-48.

[16] Ibid., 48.

[17] Ibid.

[18] Ibid.

[19] Cairns, 73.

[20] Ibid.

[21] Gary R. Habermas, *Ancient Evidence for the Life of Jesus* (Nashville: Thomas Nelson Publishers, 1984), 42.

[22] Josh McDowell and Bill Wilson, *He Walked Among Us* (San Bernardino: Here's Life Publishers, 1988), 130.

[23] Lightfoot and Harmer, 67.

[24] Ibid., 75.

[25] Ibid., 68.

[26] Ibid., 17.

[27] Ibid., 97.

[28] Ibid., 137, 139, 149, 150, 156.

[29] Ibid., 144.

[30] Ibid., 137.

[31] Ibid., 147.

[32] Ibid., 156.

[33] Ibid., 148.

[34] Cairns, 74.

[35] Lightfoot and Harmer, 180.

[36] Ibid.

[37] Ibid., 181.

[38] Ibid., 514.

[39] Ibid., 527-528.

[40] Ibid., 528.

[41] Ibid., 529.

[42] Habermas, 93.

[43] Ibid., 87-88.

[44] Ibid., 90.

[45] Ibid.

[46] Ibid., 94.

[47] Ibid., 96.

[48] Ibid., 97.

[49] Ibid., 98.

[50] Ibid., 99-100.

[51] Ibid., 100.

[52] Ibid., 90.

[53] Flavius Josephus, *The Works of Josephus,* William Whiston, trans. (Peabody: Hendrickson Publishers, 1987), 480.

[54] Habermas, 91.

[55] Ibid., 91-92.

[56] McDowell and Wilson, 168-170.

[57] Ibid., 170.

[58] Moreland, *Scaling the Secular City,* 148-149.

[59] Ibid.

[60] Ibid., 149.

[61] Josh McDowell and Don Stewart, *Handbook of Today's Religions* (San Bernardino: Here's Life Publishers, 1983), 307-308.

[62] Moreland, 149.

[63] John Hick, *The Center of Christianity* (New York: Harper and Row, Publishers, 1978), 27-29.

[64] J. P. Moreland and Michael J. Wilkins, Jesus Under Fire (Grand Rapids: Zondervan Publishing House, 1995), 2-3.

[65] McDowell, *Evidence,* 63.

[66] Roy Abraham Varghese, ed. *The Intellectuals Speak Out About God* (Dallas:

Lewis and Stanley Publishers, 1984), 267-268.

[67] Ibid., 267.

[68] Ibid., 274.

[69] McDowell, *Evidence,* 66.

[70] Varghese, 274.

[71] Ibid., 205.

CHAPTER 8

DID JESUS RISE FROM THE DEAD?

A person should not reject a miracle claim simply because it does not fit into his world view. The evidence for and against a particular miracle claim must be weighed. This chapter will examine the historical evidence for the bodily resurrection of Jesus from the dead.

The importance of Christ's resurrection should not be overlooked. The apostle Paul considered belief in Christ's resurrection to be necessary for salvation (Romans 10:9). Paul also stated:

> . . . and if Christ has not been raised, then our preaching is vain, your faith also is vain. . . and if Christ has not been raised, your faith is worthless; you are still in your sins (1 Corinthians 15:14, 17).

Paul was quick to point out that if Christ could not raise Himself from the dead, then faith in Him would be worthless. Therefore, Christianity stands or falls on the resurrection of Christ. If the resurrection really happened, then Christianity is true and Jesus is the only Savior. However, if the resurrection never occurred, then Christianity is just another false religion, promoting a false messiah.

CHRIST'S RESURRECTION WAS BODILY

Before examining the evidence for Christ's resurrection, the nature of that resurrection must be discussed. Throughout the centuries the Christian Church has recognized that Christ's resurrection was bodily.[1] Despite this fact, many today deny that Jesus rose bodily from the dead. The Jehovah's Witnesses are a non-Christian cult which denies Christ's bodily resurrection. Their literature states:

> On the third day of his being dead in the grave his immortal Father Jehovah God raised him from the dead, not as a human Son, but as a mighty immortal spirit Son, with all power in heaven and earth under the Most High God.[2]

> Jesus was the first one to rise from the dead. . . This firstborn one from the dead was not raised out of the grave a human creature, but was raised a spirit.[3]

Unfortunately, the denial of the bodily resurrection of Christ is no longer limited solely to non-Christian cults. Even evangelical scholar Murray Harris has denied that Jesus rose in the body which was crucified.[4] To make matters worse, many evangelical scholars, rather than refuting his heresy, have come to Harris' defense when he was confronted by Christian apologist Norman Geisler.[5]

If Christ did not rise bodily, then there would be no way to verify the truth of the resurrection. Presumably, His corpse would have been rotting in the tomb when the apostles were proclaiming

Him as the risen Savior. Although those who hold to a spiritual resurrection of Christ usually invent an additional miracle through which Christ's corpse dissappears, it seems more reasonable to conclude that either Jesus rose bodily or His corpse remained in the tomb. Since the New Testament records that the tomb was empty, it implies that the resurrection was bodily. A few passages of Scripture will suffice to show that Christ's resurrection, according to the apostles, was bodily:

> He is not here, for He has risen, just as He said. Come, see the place where He was lying (Matthew 28:6).

> Jesus answered and said to them, "Destroy this temple, and in three days I will raise it up." . . . But He was speaking of the temple of His body (John 2:19, 21).

> And after eight days again His disciples were inside, and Thomas with them. Jesus came, the doors having been shut, and stood in their midst, and said, "Peace be with you." Then He said to Thomas, "Reach here your finger, and see My hands; and reach here your hand, and put it into My side; and be not unbelieving, but believing" (John 20:26-27).

> And while they were telling these things, He Himself stood in their midst. But they were startled and frightened and thought that they were seeing a spirit. And He said to them, "Why are you troubled, and why do doubts arise in your

hearts? See My hands and My feet, that it is I Myself; touch Me and see, for a spirit does not have flesh and bones as you see that I have." And when He had said this, He showed them His hands and His feet. And while they still could not believe it for joy and were marveling, He said to them, "Have you anything here to eat?" And they gave Him a piece of broiled fish; and He took it and ate it before them (Luke 24:36-43).

The apostles were eyewitnesses of Christ's post-resurrection appearances. Their testimony revealed several important points. First, the tomb was empty. Second, Christ appeared to them on several occassions. Third, they thought He was a spirit. Fourth, Jesus proved to them that He was physical by inviting them to touch His body and by eating with them. Fifth, His pierced side, hands, and feet showed that His resurrection body was the body which was crucified. Therefore, it is clear that the apostles taught that Christ rose bodily. The debate about whether Christ's resurrection was bodily is usually based upon this passage:

So also is the resurrection of the dead. It is sown a perishable body, it is raised an imperishable body; it is sown in dishonor, it is raised in glory; it is sown in weakness, it is raised in power; it is sown a natural body, it is raised a spiritual body. . . (1 Corinthians 15:42-44).

THE SPIRITUAL BODY

Many people misunderstand the phrase "spiritual body." They mistake this phrase for signifying some type of immaterial spirit. However, this is not the case. In the Greek, the phrase is "soma pneumatikon." The word soma almost always refers to a physical body. Still, in this passage this physical body is somehow described as being "spiritual" (pneumatikon). But, the spiritual body is contrasted with the natural body. The natural body refers to the physical body before physical death. The Greek words for natural body are "soma psuchikon." Literally, this phrase means a "soulish body." The word soul usually carries with it the idea of immateriality, but, in this passage, it cannot. It is referring to the human body before death, and, the human body is of course physical, despite the adjective "soulish." Therefore, if the "soulish body" is physical, then there should be no difficulty viewing the "spiritual body" as also being physical. The soulish body is sown (buried) at death, but, this same body is raised as a spiritual body; it receives new powers. It is no longer a natural body; it is a supernatural body. The body is changed, but it is still the same body. For, the body that was sown (buried) is the same body that will be raised. Gary Habermas discussed Christ's spiritual body in the following words:

> . . . the Gospels and Paul agree on an important fact: the resurrected Jesus had a new spiritual body. The Gospels never present Jesus walking out of the tomb. . . when the stone is rolled away, Jesus does not walk out the way He does in apocryphal literature. He's already gone, so He presumably exited through the rock. Later He appears in buildings and then disappears at will. The Gospels clearly say that Jesus was raised in a spiritual body. It was His real body, but it was changed, including new, spiritual qualities.[6]

Paul is using the term spiritual body to contrast it with the natural body. He is making the point that Christ's body after the Resurrection (and ours too) has different characteristics to it than it did before. . . But the point is made very clearly that what is being talked about is the same body, the contrast here is not between physical body and spiritual body, but rather between the same body in different states or with different characteristics.[7]

Walter Martin, the foremost authority on non-Christian cults during his lifetime, also discussed Christ's spiritual body in his greatest work, Kingdom of the Cults:

> However, Christ had a "spiritual body" (1 Corinthians 15:50, 53) in His glorified state, identical in form to His earthly body, but immortal, and thus capable of entering the dimension of earth or heaven with no violation to the laws of either one.[8]

Therefore, Christ rose in the same body in which He lived and died. However, His body had been changed in the "twinkling of an eye" (1 Corinthians 15:50-53) so that His mortal body (a body capable of death) was glorified and became immortal (incapable of death). In His spiritual body, He can apparently travel at the speed of thought, unhindered by distance. The Bible teaches that in the first resurrection all believers will receive glorified bodies.

Believers' bodies will be changed into glorified and immortal bodies. The presence of sin will be totally removed from them (1 Corinthians 15:50-53).

Therefore, the apostles claimed that Jesus rose bodily from the dead. Since the resurrection occurred in the physical realm it could be verified; it could be proven true or false. In reference to Christ's resurrection, only four options exist: 1) the resurrection accounts may be legends, 2) the accounts may be lies, 3) the apostles may have been sincere but deceived, or 4) the apostles were telling the truth. The remainder of this chapter will determine, by process of elimination, which of these four options best explains the available evidence.

THE RESURRECTION ACCOUNTS WERE NOT LEGENDS

The resurrection accounts were not legends. The evidence presented in the last chapter clearly shows that the resurrection accounts predate even the New Testament itself. Legends usually take centuries to evolve.[9] But, as chapter seven has shown, the earliest known written resurrection accounts date back to less than twenty years after Christ's death. These accounts were ancient creeds and hymns of the first generation church (1 Corinthians 15:3-8; Romans 10:9; etc.). There is simply no way that a resurrection legend could receive universal acceptance (in order to become a hymn or creed) in the church while the apostles themselves led the church. If the resurrection account was merely a legend, the apostles would have refuted it. If the apostles chose not to refute a ficticious resurrection story, then they would have purposely perpetrated a falsehood. In that case, however, the resurrection accounts would not be legends; instead, the apostles would be liars.

The apostles knew Jesus personally. They were eyewitnesses of the events of His life and the things He taught. The apostles also led the early church. They were the authoritative witnesses to the facts concerning Christian doctrine, history, and practice. No legend could gain wide acceptance in the first generation church with the apostles in positions of authority. Since it can be shown that the resurrection accounts were not legends, some have concluded that the apostles were liars.

THE APOSTLES WERE NOT LIARS

Skeptics sometimes accuse the apostles of fabricating the resurrection accounts. One theory suggests that the apostles stole the body of Jesus from the tomb.10 In fact, this was the first attempted refutation of Christ's resurrection (Matthew 28:11-15).

Though it would be ludicrous to suggest that the apostles overpowered the Roman soldiers who guarded Jesus' tomb, this point will not be argued here. For many skeptics reject the apostolic witness concerning the guards at the tomb. Apart from the debate over whether or not the tomb was guarded, it can still be shown that the apostles were not liars. The apostles claimed that they saw Jesus risen from the dead, and, they were willing to suffer and die for for their testimony. It is clearly against human nature for men to die for what they know to be a hoax.

Death by martyrdom is probably a more accurate way to determine if someone is telling the truth than even modern lie-detector tests. William Lane Craig describes the horrible sufferings that the first generation Christians endured for their faith:

> One of the most popular arguments against this theory is the obvious sincerity of the disciples as attested by their suffering and death . . . Writing seventy years after Jesus' death, Tacitus narrates Nero's persecution about thirty years after Christ, how the Christians were clothed with the skins of wild beasts and thrown to the dogs, how others were smeared with pitch and used as human torches to illuminate the night while Nero rode about Rome in the dress of a charioteer, viewing the spectacle. The testimonies of Suetonius and Juvenal confirm the fact that within thirty-one years after Jesus' death, Christians were dying for their faith. From the writings of Pliny the Younger, Martial, Epictetus, and Marcus Aurelius, it is clear that believers were voluntarily submitting to torture and

death rather than renounce their religion. This suffering is abundantly attested in Christian writings as well.[11]

Fox's Book of Martyrs lists the deaths of eight of the twelve original apostles. James (John's brother) was put to death with the sword by order of Herod Agrippa I. The apostle Philip was crucified. Matthew (who wrote one of the Gospels) was beaten to death with an axe-shaped weapon. Andrew (Peter's brother) was crucified on an X—shaped cross. Peter (author of two epistles) was crucified upside down by order of Nero. Bartholomew was crucified. Thomas was killed when a spear was thrust through him. Simon the Zealot was crucified.[12]

Fox's Book of Martyrs also discusses the deaths of other New Testament authors. James (a half-brother of Christ and author of the epistle bearing his name) was beaten and stoned to death. Jude (another half-brother of Jesus and author of the epistle bearing his name) was crucified. Mark (author of the Gospel bearing his name) was dragged to pieces in Alexandria. Paul (who wrote thirteen or fourteen epistles) was beheaded in Rome. Luke (who wrote the Gospel named after him and Acts) was hanged on an olive tree.[13]

The apostles claimed to have seen Christ risen from the dead. They were willing to suffer and die for this claim. It is against human nature for one to die for what one knows to be a lie. Therefore, the apostles did not steal the body. They were not lying.

They were sincere. They believed that they had really seen the resurrected Lord. Hence, they were either sincere but deceived, or they were telling the truth.

THE APOSTLES WERE NOT DECEIVED

Most of today's New Testament scholars recognize that the apostles were sincere in their belief that they had seen Jesus risen from the dead. Therefore, in an attempt to explain away the resurrection, some of these scholars accept one of several theories devised to explain how the apostles were decieved into thinking they had seen the risen Lord. It is interesting to note that these theories have all been refuted by other skeptics.[14]

The swoon theory suggests that Christ never actually died on the cross. Instead, He only passed out but was mistaken for dead. Christ then, according to this view, revived in the tomb. When He visited the apostles, they mistakenly proclaimed Him as risen from the dead.[15] The swoon theory is easily refuted. The apostle John recorded in his Gospel strong evidence for Christ's death on the cross:

> The Jews therefore, because it was the day of preparation, so that the bodies should not remain on the cross on the Sabbath (for the Sabbath was a high day), asked Pilate that their legs might be broken, and that they might be taken away. The soldiers therefore came, and broke the legs of the first man, and of the other man who was crucified with Him; but coming to Jesus, when they saw that He was already dead, they did not break His legs; but one of the soldiers pierced His side with a spear, and immediately there came out blood and water (John 19:31-34).

Death by crucifixion was a horrible ordeal. To prolong the sufferings of the crucified person, a wooden block was placed under the feet to give him leverage to straighten up in order to breathe. When the Jewish authorities wanted to quicken the deaths of the victims so that they would not be on the cross during their feast days, they would have the Roman soldiers break the legs of the crucified victims. Being unable to straighten up in order to breathe, the victim would quickly die.[16]

In Christ's case, the Roman soldier saw that He was already dead. Still, being a good soldier who was conscientious about his job, he confirmed his view that Christ was dead by thrusting his spear into Christ's side. In this way, if the soldier was mistaken and Christ was actually alive, the spear wound would be fatal. The soldier, an expert in mortal combat, was surely trained in how to deliver a death blow to an enemy. Therefore, if Christ had been alive, the piercing of His side would have certainly killed Him.

Another detail in this passage provides evidence that Christ did in fact die. The apostle John reported a flow of "blood and water" coming from Christ's side as a result of the spear wound. Today, medical science has shown that this phenomenon proves that Christ was dead prior to the spear wound.[17] The flow of "blood and water" could only occur if the wound was inflicted upon a corpse. It should also be noted that this medical knowledge was unknown in John's day. Therefore, he had no knowledge that his reporting of this detail was irrefutable proof of death. Hence, he could not have fabricated this event in an attempt to prove Christ's death.[18]

The evidence, therefore, clearly indicates that Jesus died on the cross. Still, even if He did survive the cross, imminent death would follow due to His injuries from the scourging and crucifixion. Furthermore, even if He survived these injuries, there is no way in His battered condition He would have been able to convince His disciples that He had conquered death for all mankind.[19] The evidence declares that Jesus did die.

Some skeptics have proposed the wrong tomb theory. This view holds that everyone went to the wrong tomb and thus proclaimed Christ as risen.[20] However, this theory also has many problems. It offers no explanation for the apostles' claim to have seen the risen Christ on several occassions, and the apostles' willingness to die for their testimony. Also, the Jewish religious authorities would have searched every tomb in the Jerusalem area in an attempt to produce the rotting corpse of Christ. They had both the means and the desire to do so. Had they produced the corpse, Christianity would have been dealt a death blow while still in its infancy. The fact that the Jews did not produce the corpse of Christ is itself evidence of the empty tomb.[21] Again, any claim that the disciples stole the body offers no explanation as to how they could have been willing to die for what they knew to be a hoax.

Other skeptics have proposed the hallucination theory. This theory states that the apostles did not really see the resurrected Christ; instead, they only hallucinated and thought they saw the risen Lord.[22] However, psychologists inform us that hallucinations occur inside a person's mind. It is therefore impossible for two people—not to mention 500—to have had the same hallucination at the same time. Since many of the reported appearances of the risen Christ were to groups of people, the hallucination theory fails to explain the resurrection accounts.[23]

Another attempt to explain away the resurrection is the hypnotic theory. This highly speculative view suggests that the witnesses of Christ's post-resurrection appearances were all hypnotized. They did not actually see the risen Lord. Today, modern hypnotists deny this possibility.[24] Christian scholar Gary Habermas sums up the failure of skeptics to explain away the resurrection of Christ:

> One interesting illustration of this failure of the naturalistic theories is that they were disproven by the nineteenth-century older liberals themselves, by whom these views were popularized. These scholars refuted each other's theories, leaving no viable naturalistic hypotheses. For instance,

Albert Schweitzer dismissed Reimaru's fraud theory and listed no proponents of this view since 1768. David Strauss delivered the historical death blow to the swoon theory held by Karl Venturini, Heinrich Paulus, and others. On the other hand, Friedrich Schleiermacher and Paulus pointed out errors in Strauss's hallucination theory. The major decimation of the hallucination theory, however, came at the hands of Theodor Keim. Otto Pfleiderer was critical of the legendary or mythological theory, even admitting that it did not explain Jesus' resurrection. By these critiques such scholars pointed out that each of these theories was disproven by the historical facts.[25]

CONCLUSION:
THE APOSTLES WERE TELLING THE TRUTH

The failure of these theories shows that the apostles told the truth. Jesus did rise from the dead. Four facts of history add further support to the case for the resurrection of Christ from the dead. First, the apostles, who were devout Jews, changed the sabbath day from Saturday to Sunday in honor of the Lord's resurrection. Only a miracle such as the resurrection (which occurred on a Sunday) would lead them to change their sacred day of rest (a fifteen-hundred- year-old religious tradition).[26] Second, the Jewish religious leaders during the time of Christ remained silent as far as written records are concerned. Accusing the apostles of stealing the body was a failure. The punishment for Roman guards sleeping on post was death.[27] Thus, it is unlikely that well-trained Roman guards would allow a small group of Galilean fishermen to overpower them. The Jewish religious leaders, seeing the failure of their alternative explanation of the resurrection, chose not to record it in writing. The silence of the Jews provides strong evidence for the fact of the empty tomb. The Jewish religious leaders had every reason to refute the resurrection. They did not; therefore, it is safe to conclude that they could not. Third, despite the fact that the resurrection was being proclaimed right in Jerusalem (near the tomb of Christ), the new church grew rapidly. All that had to be done to disprove Christianity (which was the intention of the Jewish religious leaders) was to produce the rotting corpse of Christ. Yet, the church grew rapidly. The only explanation for this is that no one could refute the apostolic testimony to the resurrection of Christ.[28] Last, the conversion of both James and the apostle Paul can only be adequately understood as a direct consequence of the resurrection.[29] James was one of the half-brothers of Jesus. He was very skeptical about His brother's claim to be the Jewish Messiah (John 7:1-5). Anything short of seeing His brother risen from the dead would fail to explain his dramatic convesion and subsequent rise to leadership in the early church (1 Corinthians 15:7; Acts 15:13-21; Galatians 1:18-19; 2:9). Paul was originally a Pharisee and apparently the leading enemy of the church (Philippians 3:4-6; Acts 8:1-3). If one rejects the post-resurrection appearance of Christ to him on the road to Damascus, then the reason for his conversion is a mystery (Acts 9:1-9).

The evidence for Christ's resurrection is overwhelming. The empty tomb stands as a monument to Christ's victory over death, a monument that, though attacked throughout the ages, remains standing and unmoved. The empty tomb is not a silent witness: the echoing of the angel's voice can still be heard coming from it, "He is not here, for He has risen, just as He said. Come, see the place where He was lying" (Matthew 28:6).

ENDNOTES

[1] Geisler, *The Battle for the Resurrection,* 51.

[2] *Let God Be True* (Brooklyn: Watchtower Bible and Tract Society, 1946), 43.

[3] Ibid., 272.

[4] Murray Harris, *Raised Immortal: Resurrection and Immortality in the New Testament* (Grand Rapids: William B. Eerdmanns, 1985), 126.

[5] Norman L. Geisler, *In Defense of the Resurrection* (Charlotte: Quest Publications, 1991), 8-13.

[6] Gary Habermas and Anthony Flew, *Did Jesus Rise From the Dead?* (San Francisco: Harper and Row Publishers, 1987), 58.

[7] Ibid., 95.

[8] Martin, *Kingdom of the Cults,* 86.

[9] Craig, *Apologetics,* 197.

[10] Ibid., 179-180.

[11] Ibid., 175-176.

[12] John Foxe, *Foxe's Book of Martyrs* (Springdale: Whitaker House, 1981), 6-13.

[13] Ibid.

[14] Habermas and Flew, 20-21.

[15] Habermas, *Ancient Evidence for the Life of Jesus,* 54-58.

[16] Kenneth E. Stevenson and Gary R. Habermas, *Verdict on the Shroud* (Wayne: Banbury Books, 1981), 178-179.

[17] Ibid., 184.

[18] Ibid.

[19] Ibid.

[20] McDowell, *Evidence,* 255.

[21] Ibid.

[22] Gary R. Habermas, *The Resurrection of Jesus* (Lanham: University Press of America, 1984), 26-28.

[23] McDowell, *Evidence,* 249.

[24] Henry M. Morris, *Many Infallible Proofs* (El Cajon: Master Books, 1974), 94.

[25] Habermas and Flew, 20-21.

[26] Ibid., 22.

[27] McDowell, *Evidence,* 242.

[28] Craig, *Apologetics,* 178, 190.

[29] Ibid., 195-196.

CHAPTER 9

IS JESUS GOD?

The deity of Christ is hard to accept for many people. For a person to admit that Jesus is God in the flesh is to admit that he owes Him complete allegiance. Recognition of Jesus' Godhood calls for the abandonment of one's autonomy. Therefore, many people refuse to worship Jesus as God and consider Him to be merely a great human teacher. Mohandas K. Gandhi said of Christ:

> It was more than I could believe that Jesus was the only incarnate son of God. And that only he who believed in Him would have everlasting life. If God could have sons, all of us were His sons. If Jesus was like God ... then all men were like God and could be God Himself.[1]

The internationally respected theologian, John Hick, also denies Christ's deity:

> Now it used to be assumed—and in some Christian circles is still assumed—that this Jesus, who lived

in Palestine in the first third of the first century AD, was conscious of being God incarnate, so that you must either believe him or reject him as a deceiver or a megalomaniac. "Mad, bad, or God" went the argument. And of course if Jesus did indeed claim to be God incarnate, then this dilemma, or trilemma, does arise. But did he claim this? The assumption that he did is largely based on the Fourth Gospel, for it is here that Jesus makes precisely such claims. He says "I and the Father are one," "No one comes to the Father, but by me" and "He who has seen me has seen the Father." But it is no secret today, after more than a hundred years of scholarly study of the scriptures, that very few New Testament experts now hold that the Jesus who actually lived ever spoke those words, or their Aramaic equivalents. They are much more probably words put into his mouth by a Christian writer who is expressing the view of Christ which had been arrived at in his part of the church, probably two or three generations after Jesus' death. And it is likewise doubted whether the few sayings of the same kind in the other gospels are authentic words of Jesus. How, then, did this Christian deification of Jesus—which began within the first decades after his death and was essentially completed by the end of the first century—take place? Such a development is not as hard to understand in the ancient world as it would be today. . .[2]

It is interesting that Hick admits that the New Testament, quotes Jesus as claiming to be God. Second, he acknowledges that the deity of Christ was being taught within a few decades of Christ's death (which is what the creeds prove). And, third, Hick recognizes that the deity of

Christ was completely established as church doctrine by the end of the first century AD. However, by admitting these three facts, Hick is inadvertently conceding that all the available evidence points to the authenticity of Christ's claims to be God. Surely the apostles would have stopped this heresy (if indeed it was a heresy) when it started just decades after Christ's death. The Apostle John would also have opposed this teaching as it was being established as church dogma at the end of the first century AD.

Contrary to what John Hick believes, true scholarship bases its decisions on the evidence, not on mere speculation. All the available evidence points to the fact that Christ did claim to be God. The eyewitnesses who heard these claims died horrible deaths refusing to deny their validity. No liberal scholar has ever proposed an adequate explanation as to how a legend that Jesus claimed to be God could develop while the original apostles (those who personally knew Christ) were still alive and leading the new church. Legends take centuries to develope into dogma.[3] Any attempted origination of legends cannot get started while honest eyewitnesses are still alive (especially if these honest eyewitnesses hold positions of authority in the church). Therefore, liberal scholars like Hick can believe what they wish. However, to deny that Christ claimed to be God is to simply ignore all the available evidence. Liberal scholars throw out any passages of the Bible that do not agree with their antisupernaturalistic biases, but this is not true scholarship. True scholarship examines the evidence; it does not speculate as to how the evidence can be explained away. The World Book Encyclopedia is an example of the high regard in which many people esteem Jesus, while stopping short of calling Him God:

Jesus Christ was the founder of the Christian religion. Christians believe that He is the Son of God

who was sent to earth to save mankind. Even
many persons who are not Christians believe that
He was a great and wise teacher. He has probably
influenced humanity more than anyone else who
ever lived.[4]

It is not wise to call Jesus merely a great man and
teacher since He claimed to be God. For no merely great
man or wise teacher would claim to be God. If Jesus claimed
to be God, then we must view Him as either a liar, insane, or
God. There are no other alternatives, and no ignoring of the
evidence will help.

JESUS CLAIMED TO BE GOD

In chapter seven it was shown that the message
found in the New Testament is one and the same as the message of the first generation church. The ancient creeds found
in the New Testament predate the New Testament and represent the teachings of the apostles themselves.[5] Several of
these ancient creeds teach the deity of Christ (Philippians
2:5-11; Romans 10:9-10; 1 Timothy 3:16). Therefore, there
is no reason to doubt that Jesus claimed to be God. The leaders of the first generation church taught that Jesus is God,
and they were willing to die for their testimony. Hence, there
is no reason (apart from an a priori bias) to reject the claims
of deity made by Christ in the New Testament. The Jews
understood that Jesus was claiming to be God:

But He answered them, "My Father is working
until now, and I myself am working." For this
cause therefore the Jews were seeking all the more
to kill Him, because He not only was breaking the
Sabbath, but also was calling God His own Father,
making Himself equal with God (John 5:17-18).
Whenever Jesus spoke of a unique Father-Son rela-

tionship between God the Father and Himself, the Jews understood Him to be claiming equality with God the Father. Jesus spoke to the Jews in their language. He communicated to them on their terms. They understood Jesus to be claiming to be deity. If Jesus never meant to claim to be God, then He was one of the poorest communicators who ever lived. If Jesus was misunderstood by His listeners, He should have clarified His words. A clear and articulate representation of His words would have been in His best interest; He was executed for blasphemy (Mark 14:60-64).

Jesus taught that He deserved the same honor that the Father deserved:

> For not even the Father judges anyone, But He has given all judgment to the Son, in order that all may honor the Son, even as they honor the Father. He who does not honor the Son does not honor the Father who sent Him (John 5:22-23).

Since the Father is God, the honor due Him is worship. Therefore, Jesus taught that He also deserved to be worshiped. Despite the fact that the Old Testament Law forbid the worship of any being other than God (Exodus 20:1-6), Jesus accepted worship on numerous occassions (Matthew 2:11; 14:33; 28:9; John 9:38; 20:28-29). Jesus also stated:

> You are from below, I am from above; you are of this world, I am not of this world. I said therefore to you, that you shall die in your sins; for unless you believe that I am He, you shall die in your sins. . . . Truly, truly, I say to you, before Abraham was born, I am (John 8:23-24; 58).

The Jewish religious leaders understood Jesus'

claim to deity in this passage: "they picked up stones to throw at Him" (John 8:59). The comments of J. Dwight Pentecost are helpful:

> Christ affirmed, "Before Abraham was born, I am!" (v. 58). "I AM" was the name of the Self-existing God who had revealed Himself to Moses at the burning bush (Exod. 3:14). Jesus Christ was claiming to be "I AM", the Self-existent God. He was claiming eternity. To the Jews this was blasphemy.[6]

Merrill C. Tenney also elaborates on this specific claim of Christ:

> In actuality the phrase "I am" is an assertion of absolute, timeless existence, not merely of a personal identity as the English equivalent would suggest. A comparison of the use of the phrase, "I am" with self-revelation of Jehovah in the Old Testament shows that much the same terminology was employed. God, in commissioning Moses (Ex. 3:14), said: "Thus shalt thou say to unto the children of Israel, I AM hath sent me unto you." When the Jews heard Jesus say, "Before Abraham was born, I am," they took the statement to mean not priority to Abraham, but an assertion of deity. To them it was blasphemy, and they picked up stones to cast at Him.[7]

It is important to note two things about this passage. First, Jesus did not say, "Before Abraham was, I was." This would have been merely a claim to have preexisted Abraham. Though this would be a bold claim in itself, Christ actually said far more than that. Jesus was claiming that His existence is always in the present tense. In other words, He was claiming eternal existence for Himself. He was declaring himself to have absolutely no beginning. He was claiming that He was not bound by time. He was declaring Himself to be the eternal God. Second, Christ probably spoke these words in Aramaic (the common language of the Hebrews of his day). Therefore, He probably did not use the Greek words "ego eimi" for "I AM." Rather, He would have used the Hebrew "YHWH." This was the title for the eternal God. Out of reverence for God, the Jews never spoke this word. So here, Christ was not only be speaking the unspeakable title of God (YHWH), but He was using it to refer to Himself. Properly understood, this was probably Christ's most unambiguous claim to deity. The Jews clearly understood this, and for this reason they attempted to stone him. Another clear claim to deity made by Christ is the following passage:

> "I and the Father are one." The Jews took up stones again to stone Him. Jesus answered them, "I showed you many good works from the Father; for which of them are you stoning Me?" The Jews answered Him, "For a good work we do not stone You, but for blasphemy; and because You, being a man, make yourself out to be God" (John 10:30-33).

Concerning this passage, Merrill F. Unger wrote, "Jesus asserted His unity of essence with the Father, hence His unequivocal deity. . . and the Jews understood Him."[8] In this passage, Jesus clearly claimed to be equal with God the Father. Christ said that His nature is identical to that of the Father. The Jews understood Him to be calling Himself God. They later sentenced Him to death for these claims to deity.

Jesus also made other claims to deity. He said that,

"He who has seen Me has seen the Father" (John 14:9). When He prayed to the Father, He asked the Father to return to Him the glory which He and the Father shared before the universe was created (John 17:5).

The apostles were Jesus' closest associates. They were more familiar with the teachings of Christ than anyone else and they called Jesus God (Matthew 1:23; John 1:1; John 20:28; Philippians 2:6; Colossians 2:9; Titus 2:13; 2 Peter 1:1). This is further confirmation that Jesus did in fact claim to be God.

Considering the strong evidence for the reliability of the New Testament, Christ's claims to deity cannot be considered as legends. The teaching that Jesus is God predates the New Testament (as shown in the ancient creeds), and is best explained by attributing the source of this doctrine to Jesus Himself. It must be remembered that the apostles were not liars. They were sincere enough about their beliefs to die for them, and they recorded unambiguous statements made by Christ attributing deity to Himself.

The deity of Christ is not a legend. Jesus claimed to be God incarnate. Hence, one cannot consider Him to be simply a great man; for no mere man claims to be God. If Jesus is not God, then He was either a liar or insane. There are no other options.

JESUS WAS NOT A LIAR

The absurd idea that Jesus was a liar who claimed to be God can be easily refuted. For Christ is considered, even by many who reject His claim to deity, to have taught the highest standard of morality known to man. His teachings have motivated such actions as the abolition of slavery, government by the consent of the people, the modern hospital system, education for all children, and charitable programs for the needy. A liar could not have possibly encouraged these movements.

Christ has had a positive impact on mankind like no other person. It is extremely unlikely that so much good could come from a deceiver who led people astray by claiming to be God. The eyewitness accounts of the apostles display the tremendous love Christ had for people. It is not possible that a self-centered and egotistical liar could express genuine affection for his fellow man like that expressed by Christ. The question can also be asked, "Would a liar die for his lie?" It is doubtful that Jesus would lie and then suffer death by crucifixion as a consequence.

It has already been shown that the resurrection of Jesus was a historical event and not a hoax. But, why would God raise a blaspheming liar from the dead? Christ offered His resurrection as proof for His claims to deity (John 2:18-21; Matthew 12:38-40). Therefore, His resurrection proves the validity of His claims to be God. He claimed to be God and then proved it by doing what no mere man could do— He rose from the dead.

JESUS WAS NOT INSANE

Christ's claims to deity have been shown not to be legends or lies, but the possibility remains that Jesus may have been insane. Could it be that Jesus claimed to be God because He was mentally disturbed?

Often, people compare Jesus of Nazareth with other respected religious leaders. However, very few of these leaders (if any) claimed to be God in a unique sense. Some have claimed to be God, but then teach that we are all God. Jesus claimed to be God in a sense that no other man could claim to be God. Usually, when a religious leader makes a claim as bold as this, it is evidence that he is unbalanced. Charles Manson and David Koresh are two examples of this type of religious leader. The evidence for their instability is obvious. However, this is not so in the case of Jesus. He made bold claims to deity, but also backed these claims by the life He lived and the things He did.

Declaring Christ to be insane is not a common view. Nearly everyone admits that He was a great teacher, even if they reject His deity. However, insane people make lousy teachers. The teachings of Christ are not the teachings of a mad man. They are the greatest teachings ever taught by a man, and this man claimed to be God incarnate.

The miraculous life of Christ is also evidence that He was not insane. Christ gave evidence for His bold claims through His supernatural works. The apostles were eyewitnesses of these miracles. Even the enemies of Christ, the Jewish religious leaders of His day, did not deny His miracles. Instead, they stated in their Talmud that Jesus "practiced sorcery."[9] Though they rejected Jesus' message, they were forced to admit that He did supernatural works. However, the powerful influence for good that Christ has had upon mankind declares His miracles to be from God and not from Satan. Therefore, Jesus' miracles show that He was not insane. They provide strong evidence to support His claim to be God.

Another piece of evidence that shows Christ was not insane is the fact that His life and works were prophesied hundreds of years before His birth. A small fraction of the prophecies He fulfilled are listed below:

1) He was a descendant of Abraham (Genesis 12:1-3; fulfilled in Matthew 1:1-2 and Luke 3:34)

2) He was from the tribe of Judah (Genesis 49:10; fulfilled in Matthew 1:3 and Luke 3:33)

3) He was a descendant of Jesse (Isaiah 11:1; fufilled in Matthew 1:5-6 and Luke 3:32)

4) He was a descendant of David (Jeremiah 23:5; fulfilled

in Matthew 1:1, 6 and Luke 3:31)

5) He was born to a virgin (Isaiah 7:14; fulfilled in Matthew 1:18-25 and Luke 1:34-35)

6) He was born in Bethlehem (Micah 5:2; fulfilled in Matthew 2:1 and Luke 2:1-7)

7) His birth announced by a star (Numbers 24:7; fulfilled in Matthew 2:1-2)

8) His forerunner (Isaiah 40:3; fulfilled in Matthew 3:1-3 and Mark 1:2-4)

9) The specific time of His first coming (Daniel 9:24-27 predicts that the Messiah would be executed before the temple would be destroyed. The destruction of the temple occurred in 70AD. Matthew 27:1-2, 26 states that Jesus was crucified when Pilate was govenor of Judea. Pilate reigned as govenor in Judea from 26AD to 36AD.)

10) His miracles (Isaiah 35:4-6; fulfilled in Matthew 11:1-6)

11) His parables (Psalm 78:2; fulfilled in Matthew 13:3)

12) He was rejected by the Jews (Isaiah 53; fulfilled in Matthew 23:37; 27:22-25; Romans 10:1-3; 11:25)

13) He received a wide Gentile following (Isaiah 42:1-4; fulfilled in Romans 9:30-33; 11:11 and confirmed in the history of the church)

14) He was betrayed for 30 pieces of silver (Zechariah

11:12-13; fulfilled in Matthew 26:14-16)

15) He was forsaken by His disciples (Zechariah 13:7; fulfilled in Matthew 26:56)

16) He enterred Jerusalem on a donkey while receiving a king's welcome (Zechariah 9:9; fulfilled in Matthew 21:1-11)

17) He was silent before His accusers (Isaiah 53:7; fulfilled in Matthew 26:63; 27:14)

18) He was crucified (Psalm 22:16; fulfilled in Matthew 27:35)

19) Soldiers cast lots for His garments (Psalm 22:18; fulfilled in Matthew 27:35)

20) His bones were not broken (Psalm 34:20; fulfilled in John 19:31-34)

21) His side was pierced (Zechariah 12:10; fulfilled in John 19:34)

22) He was buried in a rich man's tomb (Isaiah 53:9; fulfilled in Matthew 27:57-60)

23) His resurrection from the dead (Psalm 16:10; fulfilled in Matthew 28:1-9)

24) His ascension (Psalm 68:18; fulfilled in Acts 1:9-11)

25) His position at the Father's right hand (Psalm 110:1; fulfilled in Hebrews 1:3)

As was noted earlier, these are just a few of the many prophecies that were fulfilled by Christ.[10] Even liberal scholars admit that these prophecies were recorded hundreds of years before Christ's birth. Although they deny the traditional early dates of the Old Testament books, it is almost universally accepted that the Septuagint (the Greek translation of the Hebrew Old Testament) was completed two hundred years before Christ was born.[11]

Most liberals do not consider some of the prophecies listed above as having been fulfilled by Christ. This is because these liberals a priori deny the possibility of miracles. Since they deny Christ's resurrection, they also deny that Christ fulfilled the Old Testament prophecy of the resurrection. Even if one removes the Old Testament predictions concerning the supernatural aspects of Christ's life, one is still left with the evidence from the fulfillment of prophecies of the non-supernatural aspects of Christ's life. Norman Geisler has noted that the chances of Christ fulfilling just sixteen of these prophecies by mere coincidence are 1 in 1045 (a one with forty-five zeroes after it).[12]

In fact, three of these Old Testament predictions concerning the Messiah—Daniel 9:26; Isaiah 42:4; Isaiah 53—are enough to prove that only Jesus of Nazareth meets the messianic qualifications. Daniel 9:26 stated that the Messiah would be executed before the destruction of the temple (which occurred in 70AD). Isaiah 42:4 teaches that the Gentile nations would expectantly await Christ's law. Isaiah 53 declares that the Jews would reject their Messiah. Jesus of Nazareth is the only person in history who has fulfilled all three of these prophecies. He claimed to be the Jewish Messiah and was crucified around 30AD (forty years before the temple was destroyed), the Jews rejected Him, and He received a wide Gentile following.

The life of an insane man would not be prophesied. It is also unlikely that these predictions would refer to an insane man as the Messiah (God's annointed one) and "the mighty God" (Isaiah 9:6). More than 200 years before Jesus' birth, His life and works were predicted. He fulfilled these prophecies and performed many miracles. It is absurd for someone to call Jesus insane. To accept His claims is the only reasonable response.

The historical evidence shows that Jesus claimed to be God and proved it by raising Himself from the dead. History shows these claims are not legends, and that He was not a liar, insane, or merely a great man. Therefore, Jesus of Nazareth is God.

THEREFORE, JESUS IS GOD

The following ancient creed was formulated and proclaimed by the first generation church. It declares Jesus to be God and Savior, and instructs all creation to surrender to His Lordship:

> Have this attitude in yourselves which was also in Christ Jesus, who, although He existed in the form of God, did not regard equality with God a thing to be grasped, but emptied Himself, taking the form of a bond-servant, and being made in the likeness of men. And being found in appearance as a man, He humbled Himself by becoming obedient to the point of death, even death on a cross. Therefore also God highly exalted Him, and bestowed on Him the name which is above every name, that at the name of Jesus every knee should bow, of those who are in heaven, and on earth, and under the earth, and that every tongue should confess that Jesus Christ is Lord, to the glory of God the Father (Philippians 2:5-11).

This ancient creed states that the day will come

when all creation will bow down before Christ and confess that He is Lord. One can bow to Jesus now, or one can bow to Jesus later, but, the fact remains, that the day will come when all will bow before Christ, both the saved and the unsaved. The saved will bow before Jesus to worship Him as their Savior and King. The lost will bow before Him, due to their fear of His power and authority.

ENDNOTES

[1] Mohandas K. Gandhi, *Mahatma Gandhi Autobiography* (Washington, D. C.: Public Affairs Press, 1948), 170.

[2] Hick, *The Center of Christianity,* 27-28.

[3] Wilkins and Moreland, eds., 154.

[4] *The World Book Encyclopedia,* vol. 11, (Chicago: World Book, Inc., 1985), 82.

[5] Moreland, *Scaling the Secular City,* 148-149.

[6] J. Dwight Pentecost, *The Words and Works of Jesus Christ* (Grand Rapids: Academie Books, 1981), 288.

[7] Merrill C. Tenney, *John, the Gospel of Belief* (Grand Rapids: William B. Eerdmans Publishing Company, 1948), 150.

[8] Merrill F. Unger, *Unger's Bible Handbook* (Chicago: Moody Press, 1966), 555.

[9] Habermas, *Ancient Evidence for the Life of Jesus,* 98.

[10] For a fuller treatment of Old Testament prophecies fulfilled by Christ, see: Josh McDowell, *Evidence,* 141-177.

[11] Ibid.,144.

[12] Geisler, *Apologetics,* 343.

CHAPTER 10

IS THE BIBLE GOD'S WORD?

The preceding chapters have provided strong evidence for the historical reliability of the Bible, as well as for the resurrection and deity of Christ. In this chapter, evidence showing the Bible to be God's Word will be examined. The case for the inspiration of the Scriptures builds upon the evidence produced in the last four chapters.

CHRIST'S TEACHINGS CONCERNING THE OLD TESTAMENT

This work has shown that the evidence demonstrates that Jesus is God. Therefore, whatever Jesus taught should be accepted as true and authoritative. John W. Wenham discussed Christ's view of the Old Testament:

Our Lord not only believed the truth of the Old Testament history and used the Scriptures as final authority in matters of faith and conduct, he also regarded the writings themselves as inspired. To

Him, Moses, the prophets, David, and the other Scripture writers were given their messages by the Spirit of God.[1]

Some of Christ's teachings concerning the Old Testament are as follows:

Do not think that I came to abolish the Law or the Prophets; I did not come to abolish, but to fulfill. For truly I say to you, until heaven and earth pass away, not the smallest letter or stroke shall pass away from the Law, until all has been accomplished (Matthew 5:17-18).

And He answered and said to them, "And why do you yourselves transgress the commandment of God for the sake of your tradition? For God said, 'Honor your father and mother,' and, 'He who speaks evil of father or mother, let him be put to death' " (Matthew 15:3-4).

But regarding the resurrection of the dead, have you not read that which was spoken to you by God, saying, "I am the God of Abraham, and the God of Isaac, and the God of Jacob"? (Matthew 22:31-32).

He was also saying to them, "You nicely set aside the commandment of God in order to keep your tradition. For Moses said, 'Honor your father and your mother'; and, 'He who speaks evil of father or mother, let him be put to death'; but you say, 'If a man says to his father or mother, anything of mine you might have been helped by is Corban (that is to say, given to God),' you no longer permit him to do anything for his father or his mother; thus invalidating the word of God by your tradition which you have handed down. . ." (Mark 7:9-13).

David himself said in the Holy Spirit, "The Lord said to my Lord, 'Sit at My right hand, until I put Thine enemies beneath Thy feet' " (Mark 12:36).

It is abundantly clear that Jesus considered the entire Old Testament (what the Jews of His day called "the Law and the Prophets") to be the inspired Word of God. He referred to the Old Testament authors as prophets (Matthew 11:13; 12:39; 22:40; 23:31-35; 24:15; 26:56; Luke 16:16-17, 31; 18:31; 24:44; John 6:45), meaning proclaimers of God's truth. In fact, Jesus spoke of the prophets as beginning with Abel and ending with Zechariah (Luke 11:49-51). This covers the exact time period of the Old Testament, from creation to about 400BC. Since Christ is God Himself, his view of the Old Testament must be correct. Therefore, the Old Testament is the written Word of God.

CHRIST'S VIEW OF THE NEW TESTAMENT
Christ ascended to heaven before the New Testament was recorded. However, the promises He made to his apostles guaranteed that the New Testament would be the inspired Word of God:

Go therefore and make disciples of all nations, baptizing them in the name of the Father and the Son and the Holy Spirit, teaching them to observe all that I commanded you; and lo, I am with you always, even to the end of the age (Matthew 28:19-20).

Heaven and earth will pass away, but My words will not pass away (Mark 13:31).

But the Helper, the Holy Spirit, whom the Father will send in My name, He will teach you all things, and bring to your remembrance all that I said to you (John 14:26).

When the Helper comes, whom I will send to you from the Father, that is the Spirit of truth, who proceeds from the Father, He will bear witness of Me, and you will bear witness also, because you have been with Me from the beginning (John 15:26-27).

But when He, the Spirit of truth, comes, He will guide you into all the truth; for He will not speak on His own initiative, but whatever He hears, He will speak; and He will disclose to you what is to come (John 16:13).

But you shall receive power when the Holy Spirit has come upon you; and you shall be My witnesses both in Jerusalem, and in all Judea and Samaria, and even to the remotest part of the earth (Acts 1:8).

From these quotes of Christ, five conclusions can be drawn. First, Jesus promised that His teachings would be preserved. Second, He said that the Holy Spirit would remind the apostles of all that He told them. Third, the Holy Spirit would reveal future events to the apostles. Fourth, the Holy Spirit would guide the apostles into the truth (prevent them from promoting doctrinal errors). Fifth, the Holy Spirit would empower the apostles to be Christ's authoritative representatives to the world.

From the above conclusions it is clear that Christ promised to preserve His teachings through the apostles' writings. Obviously, these writings make up the New Testament. Since Jesus is almighty God, His plan cannot be thwarted. Therefore, since He promised to preserve His words through the teachings of the apostles, then their teachings (which have been passed on to future generations) are the teachings of Christ. Hence, they are the Word of God.

It should also be noted that Jesus taught that only the Old Testament and the teachings of His apostles (the New Testament) were the Word of God. The evidence declares Jesus to be God. Jesus taught that both the Old and New Testaments are the Word of God. Therefore, the Old and New Testaments are the Word of God.

THE SUPERNATURAL WISDOM OF THE BIBLE

The evidence presented above is sufficient to demonstrate that the Bible is God's Word. Still, there are other factors which help corroborate this evidence. The supernatural wisdom and the fulfilled prophecies of the Bible verify that the Bible is God's Word.

Christian thinkers such as Blaise Pascal (1623-1662)[2] and Francis Schaeffer (1912-1984)[3] have noted that only the Bible offers an adequate explanation for both man's greatness and man's wretchedness. Modern man, even with all his accumulated knowledge, cannot sufficiently account for both aspects in man. Atheistic evolutionists may be able to explain the wretchedness of man, for they see man as merely an animal, but they cannot satisfactorily account for man's greatness. New Age Pantheists recognize man's greatness by attributing godhood to him, but, they offer no convincing reason why man is so wretched. The Bible alone offers an adequate explanation for both aspects of man. Man is great because he was created in

God's image; he is wretched because he is in a fallen state.[4] This indicates that the wisdom found in the Bible supersedes the wisdom of man.

Evidence for the supernatural wisdom of the Bible can also be seen in the realm of science. At a time when men thought the earth was flat, the Bible taught that it was a sphere (Isaiah 40:22, 700BC). At a time when men thought the earth rested on the back of a giant turtle, the Bible taught that is was suspended in space (Job 26:7, 2000BC). At about 1500BC the Bible taught that the stars could not be counted (Genesis 15:5); yet, in 150AD an astronomer named Ptolemy taught that there were exactly 1056 stars.[5] Today, modern science confirms that the stars are innumerable.

In about 1850AD, the first and second laws of thermodynamics were discovered by modern science. The first law teaches that no new energy is being created or destroyed. The second law teaches that, though the amount of energy in the universe remains constant, the amount of usable enrgy is running down. Therefore, the universe is winding down. The Bible taught both of these laws thousands of years ago. The Bible states that God is resting from His creation work (Genesis 2:1-3), and that the universe will someday pass away (Mark 13:31; Isaiah 40:31). The Bible does teach, however, that God will make a new heaven and a new earth when the old ones pass away (Revelation 21:1).

There was no such thing as modern science in biblical times. Hence, the information mentioned above demands a source which transcends that of man, a supernatural source.[6] H. L. Willmington commented on this subject:

> In 1861 the French Academy of Science published a brochure of fifty-one "scientific facts" which supposedly contradicted the Bible. These were used by the atheists of that day in ridiculing Christians. Today all fifty-one of those "facts" are

UNacceptable to modern scientists.[7]

FULFILLED PROPHECIES

The Bible claims repeatedly to be the Word of God. One of the most powerful witnesses to the truth of this claim is the many fulfilled prophecies proclaimed in the Bible. This work has already examined a sample of prophecies fulfilled by Christ. Here, a few more of the many biblical prophecies that have already come to pass will be discussed.

The Bible has made many predictions concerning the future of great nations and cities. The following is a brief discussion of a few of the prophecies fulfilled concerning these cities and nations.

Around 590—570BC, the prophet Ezekiel predicted that the city of Tyre would be destroyed and never be rebuilt, and that it would become a barren rock which fishermen would use to mend their nets (Ezekiel 26:4, 5, 14). Though Tyre was destroyed and rebuilt many times throughout history, it was ultimately devestated in 1291AD by Muslim invaders. Today, all that is left of the ancient site of Tyre is a small fishing community which uses the barren ground to dry their nets.[8]

In the sixth century BC, Ezekiel also predicted that the city of Sidon would suffer much violence and bloodshed throughout her history, yet remain in existence (Ezekiel 28:23). Though Sidon has been invaded and defeated numerous times throughout her history, the city still exists today.[9]

In 625BC, the prophet Zephaniah predicted that the city of Ashkelon would someday be destroyed, but that it would eventually be inhabited by the Jews (Zephaniah 2:4, 6). Ashkelon was destroyed in 1270AD by Sultan Bibars. The city remained unihabited for centuries until the nation of Israel was reestablished in 1948. Now, the Jews have rebuilt and reinhabited Ashkelon.[10]

Zephaniah also predicted that the Philistines—a powerful enemy of the Jews throughout much of the Old Testament—would be totally wiped out. Though they continued to prosper for many centuries, they eventually became extinct in 1200AD (Zephaniah 2:5).[11]

The prophet Obadiah, writing in either 841BC or 586BC, prophesied the extinction of the Edomites, who were the descendants of Esau and enemies of the Jews (Obadiah 18). When the Romans devestated the city of Jerusalem in 70AD, they also defeated the remnants of Edom (called the Idumeans at that time). At that time, all traces of the Edomites disappear.[12]

In 740—680BC, the prophet Isaiah predicted that Egypt would still be a nation in the last days (Isaiah 19:21-22). In spite of the many wars Egypt has encountered throughout her four-thousand year history, this ancient nation remains in existence to this day.[13]

In 1410BC, Moses predicted that Israel would be scattered among the nations of the world (Deuteronomy 28:64). The prophet Hosea, in 710BC, predicted this dispersion of Israel as well (Hosea 9:17). History records that after the Romans destroyed Jerusalem, the Jews were scattered throughout the world.[14]

Both Isaiah and Ezekiel prophesied that Israel would be regathered in her land in the last days (Isaiah 11:11-12; Ezekiel 37:21). This happened in 1948AD when the nation of Israel was reestablished. The Jews continue to return to their land to this day.[15]

God told Abraham that those who cursed Israel would be cursed by God (Genesis 12:3). This prophecy has been fulfilled many times. Babylon, Assyria, Philistia, the Roman Empire, and Nazi Germany are a few examples of nations or empires that persecuted and oppressed Israel. While the tiny nation of Israel still exists today, Babylon, Assyria, Philistia, the Roman Empire, the Soviet Union, and

Nazi Germany have collapsed and are no longer in existence. During the 1930's and 1940's, Nazi Germany had slaughtered six-million Jews and its war machine was devestating Europe. By 1948, Nazi Germany was nonexistent and the Jews had control of their homeland—the nation of Israel— for the first time since 586BC.[16]

Each of these prophecies has been fulfilled to the detail. Many other biblical prophecies have also been fulfilled. It should also be noted that no futuristic prophecy of Scripture has ever been shown to be false. This separates the Bible from false prophets such as Edgar Cayce and Jean Dixon. Their success rate is much lower than the perfect accuracy of the predictions made by the Bible.[17] Henry Morris made the following comment:

> It seems reasonable to conclude that the phenomenon of fulfilled prophecy constitutes a unique and powerful evidence of the divine inspiration of the Bible.[18]

The evidence provided above for the Bible being God's Word is threefold. First, Jesus (who is God) taught that the Bible is God's Word. Second, the Bible contains insights that go beyond mere human wisdom. Third, the Bible made numerous predictions, many of which have been fulfilled. None of these predictions have proven false (though some prophecies have yet to be fulfilled). In short, there are good reasons for believing the Bible is God's Word. Those who reject the divine inspiration of the Bible have failed to explain the three factors above.

IMPLICATIONS OF THE DIVINE INSPIRATION OF THE BIBLE

Since the Bible can be shown to be God's Word, several implications follow. First, since the cosmological argument has shown God to be infinite and perfect, there can be no error in His Word as originally recorded. God can only proclaim truth; otherwise, He would be less than perfect. Therefore, the Bible is wholly true (inerrant). Second, since the Bible is God's inerrant Word, it is authoritative. God has spoken, and everything must be tested by the truth He has given. Third, whatever is taught in God's inerrant and authoritative Word should be adhered to by all.

This work has already presented evidence for some of the major tenets of orthodox Christianity (the existence of one God, creation by God, the resurrection of Jesus, and Christ's deity). Since the evidence indicates the Bible is God's Word, whatever it teaches must be true. Therefore, other important Christian doctrines (e.g., salvation by grace through faith in Christ, the substitutionary death of Christ, the Trinity, and Christ's future return to earth) can be defended by showing that they are taught in the Bible.

Concerning salvation, the Bible teaches that all people are sinners who cannot save themselves (Romans 3:10, 23; 6:23; Matthew 19:25-26). Scripture teaches that man cannot earn his salvation; salvation is a free gift given by God's grace (unmerited favor) to those who trust (believe) in Jesus for salvation (Ephesians 2:8-9; John 3:16-18; 6:35, 47; Romans 6:23). Only through Jesus can man be saved (John 14:6; Acts 4:12).

The Bible teaches that Jesus took mankind's punishment upon Himself by dying on the cross for our sins (Isaiah 53:5-6, 12; Matthew 1:21; Mark 10:45; John 1:29; Romans 5:8-10; Ephesians 1:7; 2 Corinthians 5:15, 21; 1 Timothy 2:4-6; Hebrews 10:10, 14; 1 Peter 2:24; 3:18; 1 John 1:7; 2:1-2; Revelation 5:9). The God of the Bible is holy and just; He cannot forgive sin unless it has been paid for in full. The good news is that Jesus (who is fully man and fully God) is the ultimately worthy sacrifice who has paid for the sins of the world through His death on the cross (Revelation 5:1-

14). He died as a substitute for all of mankind. Those who accept Jesus as their Savior receive the salvation and forgiveness that He has purchased for them.

One of the most controversial teachings of Christianity is the doctrine of the Trinity, for this teaching transcends human understanding. This doctrine declares that the one true God eternally exists as three equal Persons (the Father, Son, and Holy Spirit). God is one in essence or nature (Mark 12:29; John 10:30), but three in Personhood (Matthew 3:16-17; John 14:16, 26; 15:26).

The Bible teaches that the Father is God (Galatians 1:1; 1 Peter 1:2). However, Jesus (the Son) is also called God and is described in ways that could only apply to God (Isaiah 9:6; Zechariah 14:5; John 1:1, 14; 5:17-18, 22-23; 8:58-59; 10:30-33; 17:5, 24; 20:28; Romans 9:5; Colossians 2:9; Titus 2:13; Hebrews 1:8; 2 Peter 1:1; 1 John 5:20; Revelation 1:17-18). Jesus is worshiped as God (Matthew 2:11; 28:9; John 9:38). The Holy Spirit is also called God (Acts 5:3-4; 1 Corinthians 3:16).

Some have speculated that the Father, Son, and Holy Spirit, since they are one God, must also be one Person, but, this is not what the Bible teaches. The Bible teaches that the Father, Son, and Holy Spirit are three distinct Persons (Isaiah 48:12-16; Psalm 110:1; Matthew 3:16-17; 28:19; John 14:16, 26; 15:26). Before anything was created, the three Persons of the Trinity communicated with each other (Genesis 1:26; 11:7), shared the glory of God (John 17:5), and loved each other (John 17:24). Even while Christ was on earth, He and the Father spoke to one another, thus proving they were not the same Person (Matthew 3:16-17; 26:39; Luke 23:46; John 17:1). When all the data is considered, it is clear that the Bible teaches that there is only one true God, but this God eternally exists as three equal Persons. Hence, the Bible teaches the doctrine of the Trinity.

The Bible also teaches that Jesus Christ will someday

return to earth in power and glory. After His return, He will rule over the nations for one-thousand years (Matthew 24:29-31; Revelation 11:15; 19:11-16; 20:4-6).

Since the available evidence declares the Bible to be God's Word, whatever it teaches must be true. Therefore, the biblical teachings concerning salvation, Christ's substitutionary death, the Trinity, and Christ's return should be accepted. It is also important to note that since whatever the Bible teaches is true, the morality taught in the Bible is authoritative. If God calls a practice wrong, then it is wrong, regardless of common political sentiment. Though the Bible student must differentiate between absolute moral laws which are universally binding on all men and temporary cultural laws prescribed for a specific people at a specific time, absolute moral laws taught in the Bible should be adhered to by all. The day will come when all must answer to God at the final judgment (2 Corinthians 5:10; Revelation 20:11-15).

CONCLUSION

The argument of this chapter is threefold. First, Jesus of Nazareth, who is God incarnate, taught that the Bible is God's Word. Therefore, the Bible is the Word of God. Second, this is confirmed by the supernatural wisdom of the Bible, as well as the many fulfilled prophecies of the Bible. Third, since God has been shown to be infinitely perfect, His Word is totally trustworthy. Therefore, whatever the Bible teaches is true.

Since the Bible teaches that salvation comes only through trusting in Jesus as one's Savior, then Christianity is the one true faith. All religions which deny salvation only through Christ alone are false religions. One's eternal destiny depends on his response to Christ. It is Jesus who calls out to all mankind, "Come to Me, all who are weary and heavy-laden, and I will give you rest" (Matthew 11:28).

POSTSCRIPT: A GENERAL APOLOGETIC AGAINST ALL NON-CHRISTIAN RELIGIONS

Christian apologists, when dealing with non-Christian religions, must defend the essential Christian beliefs as this work has done, as well as refute the doctrines that are proclaimed by the religion in question. In closing this work, three points should be made regarding the superiority of the Christian faith.

First, the God of Christianity is more just than the supposed gods of the world religions, for the God of the Bible cannot forgive sin unless it has been paid for in full (Romans 3:21-26). He cannot ignore or overlook sin. The God of Christianity demands the ultimate penalty (the eternal flames of hell) for rebellion against Him. Only the ultimately worthy sacrifice (the death of Jesus) can atone for the sins of mankind. The non-Christian world religions, on the other hand, either attempt to explain away the reality of sin and guilt, or accept the reality of sin, but downplay its severity so that man can atone for his own sins.

Second, the God of Christianity is more loving than the gods of the world religions. His justice demands that He punish all sin, but His love caused Him to go to the cross to die for the sins of mankind (1 Peter 2:24; 3:18; John 3:16; Romans 5:8). God became a man (John 1:1, 14; Philippians 2:5-8) and took the punishment for mankind. The ultimately worthy sacrifice (Jesus) was offered as a substitute for the sins of all people. However, God's love cannot be forced upon anyone. Forced love is not love; it is rape. Though Jesus paid the price for the sins of mankind, God gives each person the freedom to accept or reject His forgiveness and salvation by accepting or rejecting Jesus as Savior. God desires to save every person (Matthew 23:37; 1 Timothy 2:1-6; 2 Peter 3:9), but as a God of love, He will not force His will on His creatures.

Third, the Christian salvation message makes more

sense than the salvation messages proclaimed in non-Christian world religions. All the major world religions teach that limited and imperfect man can reach the unlimited and perfect God on his own. However, it is impossible for a limited being, on its own, to reach an unlimited Being. Christianity teaches that if man is to be saved, it must be accomplished by the unlimited God Himself. When the disciples asked Jesus how man could be saved, He responded, "With men this is impossible, but with God all things are possible" (Matthew 19:25-26). Therefore, man must look to God for salvation. Salvation is by God's grace alone (Ephesians 2:8-9); it is not earned through human effort.

Christianity is the one true faith. It differs from all other world religions on essential matters. Therefore, Christianity and the world religions cannot both be true. If Christianity is true, all other religions are false.

ENDNOTES

[1] Norman L. Geisler, ed., *Inerrancy* (Grand Rapids: Academie Books, 1980), 16-17.

[2] Pascal, 56-61.

[3] Schaeffer, *Complete Works,* vol. 1, 293-304.

[4] Pascal, 56-61.

[5] H. L. Willmington, *That Manuscript From Outer Space* (Nashville: Thomas Nelson Publishers, 1974), 99.

[6] Ibid.

[7] Ibid., 108.

[8] McDowell, *Evidence,* 270-280.

[9] Ibid., 280-281.

[10] Ibid., 283-285.

[11] Morris, *Many Infallible Proofs,* 183.

[12] Tenney, *The Zondervan Pictorial Bible Dictionary,* 233-234.

[13] Morris, *Many Infallible Proofs,* 182.

[14] Ibid., 186-187.

[15] Ibid., 187-188.

[16] Ibid., 186.

[17] The predictions of Scripture are always clear in their meaning and no prophecy of Scripture has ever been shown to be inaccurate. On the other hand, the prophecies of Edgar Cayce and Jeane Dixon have been shown to be extremely vague and often inaccurate. Specific cases of false prophecies uttered by Cayce and Dixon are documented in Josh McDowell and Don Stewart, *Handbook of Today's Religions,* 169-174, 181-185. According to Deuteronomy 18:22, one failed prophecy is enough to identify a person as a false prophet. Hence, both Cayce and Dixon are false prophets while, as mentioned above, no prediction of the Bible has been shown to be false.

[18] Morris, *Many Infallible Proofs,* 198-199.

GORDON CLARK'S DOGMATIC PRESUPPOSITIONALISM

G ordon Haddon Clark (1902-1985) was one of the greatest Christian thinkers of the twentieth century. He was the Chairman of the Philosophy Department at Baylor University for 28 years.[1] He and Cornelius Van Til, although they disagreed on many points, were the two leading proponents of the presuppositional method of apologetics. In this chapter, Clark's apologetic methodology will be examined, and its strengths and weaknesses will be discussed.

CLARK'S REJECTION OF TRADITIONAL APOLOGETICS

Gordon Clark rejected the idea that unaided human reason could arrive at truths about God. Due to this fact, he rejected traditional apologetics. Clark stated that "The cosmological argument for the existence of God, most fully developed by Thomas Aquinas, is a fallacy. It is not possible to begin with sensory experience and proceed by the formal laws of logic to God's existence as a conclusion."[2] After listing several reasons why he rejected the Thomistic arguments for God's existence, Clark added that even if the arguments were valid, they would only prove the existence of a lesser god, not the true God of the Bible.[3]

Clark not only despised the use of philosophical arguments to provide evidence for God's existence, but he also deplored the utilization of historical evidences in defense of Christianity. Clark reminded his readers that the facts of history do not come with their own built-in interpretation. He stated that "Significance, interpretation, evaluation is not given in any fact; it is an intellectual judgment based on some non-sensory criterion."[4]

Clark declared that while the conclusions of science constantly change, scriptural truth remains the same.[5] Therefore, believers should not rely on observable facts to prove Christianity. Instead, Christians must presuppose the truth of God's Word and allow revelation to interpret the facts of history for them.[6]

The reason behind Clark's distaste for traditional apologetics was his belief that unaided human reason could never discover any truth, religious or secular. This, Clark believed, should convince a person of his need to presuppose the truth of the Christian revelation.[7] Without this presupposition, man cannot find truth. Clark emphasized this point at the conclusion of his textbook on the history of philosophy. He stated, "Does this mean that philosophers and cultural epochs are nothing but children who pay their fare to take another ride on the merry-go-round? Is this Nietzsche's eternal recurrence? Or, could it be that a choice must be made between skeptical futility and a word from God?"[8]

CLARK'S REJECTION OF EMPIRICISM

Empiricism is the attempt to find truth through the five senses. This school of thought believes "that all knowledge begins in sense experience."[9]

According to Clark, Thomas Aquinas was an empiricist. Aquinas believed that "all knowledge must be abstracted out of our sensations."[10] Aquinas believed that each person begins life with his mind as a blank slate. He held that "everything that is in the mind was first in the senses, except the mind itself."[11] Although Aquinas believed that God created man's mind with the innate ability to know things and draw rational conclusions from sense data, Clark does not seem to do justice to this aspect of Aquinas' thought.[12] Instead, he merely attacks the idea that man could argue from sense data to the existence of God.

Clark turns next to William Paley. Paley argued from the evidence of design in the universe to the existence of an intelligent God as its Cause. Therefore, he, like Aquinas, began with sense experience and then argued to the existence of God. Clark agreed with the criticisms made by David Hume concerning the teleological argument (the argument for God's existence from design). Hume stated that experience cannot determine if there was one God or several gods who designed the world. Second, since the physical world is finite, nothing in man's experience tells him that its designer must be infinite. And third, since human experience includes such things as natural disasters, might not the world's designer be an evil being?[13]

Clark pointed out that Hume himself was an empiricist. But Hume was consistent in his thinking. Therefore, he realized that the principle of cause and effect, the existence of external bodies, and the reality of internal selves could not be proven through sense data alone. Therefore, Hume admitted that his empiricism inevitably led to skepticism.[14]

Clark emphasized the point that there is a wide gap between basic sense experience and the propositional conclusions made by empiricists.[15] Sense data (the facts of experience) do not come with their own built-in interpretation.

Rational conclusions cannot come from sense experience alone. Empiricism, therefore, fails as a truth-finding method. Next, Gordon Clark turned his attention to rationalism.

CLARK'S REJECTION OF RATIONALISM

Rationalism is the attempt to find truth through reason alone. Though Clark admitted that Augustine was not a pure rationalist, he discussed his views of reason.[16] At a time when Greek philosophy was dominated by skepticism, which argued against the possibility of attaining knowledge, Augustine attempted to find a base for knowledge that could not be denied.[17] Augustine declared that "the skeptic must exist in order to doubt his own existence."[18] Augustine therefore reasoned that even the skeptic should be certain of his existence. Augustine also showed that skeptics could not live like knowledge was impossible.[18]

Augustine also held that the laws of logic were universal, eternal, and unchanging truths. Since the human mind is limited and changing, it could not be the ultimate source of these eternal truths. Hence, there must be an eternal and unchanging Mind as their source. Obviously, this eternal Mind is God.[19]

Clark critiqued the views of Anselm. Anselm was even more rationalistic in his thought than Augustine. He believed that the existence of God could be proven through reason alone. Anselm referred to God as the greatest conceivable Being. Therefore, if God does not exist, then one could conceive of a being greater than Him, a being that has the same attributes but does exist. But then this would be the greatest conceivable Being. Therefore, God (the greatest conceivable Being) must necessarily exist.[20] This is called the ontological argument for God's existence.

Clark wrote that Rene Descartes, also a rationalist, viewed sensation and experience as very deceptive. He attempted to find a single point of certainty by doubting everything until he found something he could not doubt. Through this process, he realized that the more he doubted, the more certain he became of the existence of himself, the doubter.[21]

Descartes borrowed Anselm's ontological argument for God's existence. Clark stated Descartes' version of this argument as follows: "God, by definition, is the being who possesses all perfections; existence is a perfection; therefore God exists."[22]

Clark related that Spinoza also used the ontological argument for God's existence. But Spinoza's version of the argument did not conclude with the God of the Bible. Instead he "proved" the existence of a god who is the universe (the god of pantheism).[23] However, this raised questions as to rationalism's claim to prove the existence of God with certainty, for Spinoza's god and Descartes' God cannot bothexist. Spinoza was also more consistent in his rationalism than was Descartes. Spinoza realized that if all knowledge could be found through reason alone, then supernatural revelation is without value.[24]

Gordon Clark listed several problems with rationalism in his writings. He stated that rationalism has historically led to several contradictory conclusions (theism, pantheism, and atheism).[25] Also, Clark stated that "rationalism does not produce first principles out of something else: The first principles are innate . . . Every philosophy must have its first principles . . . Thus a presuppositionless description is impossible."[26] Although Clark made much use of reason in his own defense of the faith, he presupposed his first principles. He contended that without doing this, reason can never get off the ground.[27]

CLARK'S REJECTION OF IRRATIONALISM

In discussing the history of philosophy, Clark stated that "Hume had reduced empiricism to skepticism."[28]

Immanuel Kant's views left man with a knowledge of "things-as-they-appear-to-us," but with no real knowledge of "things-in-themselves."[29] Clark emphasized this point with the following words: "In his view the uninformed sense data are entirely incoherent. Order is introduced into them by the mind alone, and what the real world might be like. . . remains unknowable. The whole Postkantian development from Jacobi to Hegel convicts Kant of skepticism."[30]

Clark added that though Hegel effectively critiqued Kant, Hegelianism also failed to justify knowledge.[31] In Hegel's theory of the unfolding of history, truth was seen as relative. What was true yesterday is not necessarily true today.[32] In short, the greatest minds the world has ever known have failed to escape skepticism. The philosophy of man cannot even prove that man can know anything. Empiricism and rationalism have both failed. This has caused some thinkers to accept irrationalism as the method of finding meaning to life. One such thinker was Soren Kierkegaard.

Kierkegaard denied the effectiveness of both reason and sense experience in finding truth. He believed that a man must stop reasoning. Only through a blind leap of faith can man find true meaning in life. An individual's subjective passion is of more importance than objective truth. Kierkegaard believed that the doctrines of Christianity were absurd and contradictory. Still, he chose to believe against all reason.[33]

Clark rejected the irrationalism of Kierkegaard even though it had become so widespread among modern thinkers, both secular and religious. Clark stated of Kierkegaard, "The fatal flaw is his rejection of logic. When once a man commits himself to contradictions, his language, and therefore his recommendations to other people, become meaningless."[34]

As shown above, Gordon Clark rejected empiricism,

rationalism, and irrationalism. He taught that they all eventually reduce to skepticism. Man has failed to find truth through these methodologies. Therefore, man, according to Clark, must make a choice between skepticism and a word from God.[35] Clark's method of finding truth is called presuppositionalism or dogmatism.

CLARK'S VIEW: DOGMATISM

When one finds that Clark saw all of secular philosophy as unable to justify knowledge, one might assume that Clark was himself a skeptic. But this was not the case. Skeptical futility is not the only option left. Clark referred to his view of finding truth as dogmatism. Clark argued that if all other philosophical systems cannot give meaning to life, then dogmatism is worth a try. Clark recommended that one dogmatically presuppose the truth of the teachings of Scripture.[36]

Clark's view may seem to some to be fideism. But this is not so (according to Clark). For everyone, no matter what their philosophical system may be, must presuppose something.[37] The rationalist must presuppose his first principles. Otherwise, he must look for reasons for everything. This would result in an infinite regress, and there would be no real base for knowledge.[38]

The empiricist must assume certain concepts which he cannot prove through sense experience. Such concepts as time, space, equality, causality, and motion are not derived from sense experience. They are brought into one's sense experience in the beginning to aid one in drawing conclusions from the sense data.[39] Logical Positivism is an extreme empirical view. One of its first principles is that truth can only be found through the five senses. However, this first principle refutes itself since it cannot itself be proven through the five senses.[40]

Clark argued that since rationalism and empiricism

have failed to make life meaningful, Christian presuppositions should be utilized. For Christian presuppositions do give meaning to life.[41] Clark argued that "Christian Theism is self-consistent and that several other philosophies are inconsistent, skeptical, and therefore erroneous."[42] Clark added that Christianity "gives meaning to life and morality, and that it supports the existence of truth and the possibility of knowledge."[43]

One can see Clark's point more clearly by examining his critique of Kant. In Kant's thinking, there existed no order in sense data. Instead the mind introduces this order into the sense data. Therefore, Kant's view collapses into skepticism since one can only know things-as-they-appear-to-us and not things-as-they-are. One cannot know the real world. One can only know the world as it appears to him.[44]

Clark's response to Kant's dilemma is as follows. Clark presupposes the truth of the revelation found in Scripture. Therefore, Clark presupposes that "God has fashioned both the mind and the world so that they harmonize."[45] If one presupposes the truth of Christianity, then the order that the mind innately reads into the real world is the order which really exists in the real world.

Having discussed Clark's view of obtaining knowledge, one must now consider how Clark defended Christianity. Clark did this by convincing the nonbeliever that he is contradicting himself.[46] Clark was willing to use logic (the law of noncontradiction) to refute the belief systems of others. He did not feel that he was being inconsistent with his presuppositionalism or dogmatism, for Clark believed that God is Logic. In other words, logic is God-thinking. It flows naturally from God's Being.[47] In fact, Clark even translated John 1:1 as, "In the beginning was Logic, and Logic was with God, and Logic was God."[48]

The problem with rationalism is that it lacks sufficient first principles. But, according to Clark, once one presupposes the truth of the Bible, one can use reason to tear down the views of others. Clark spoke of reason in the following manner:

> Therefore I wish to suggest that we neither abandon reason nor use it unaided; but on pain of skepticism acknowledge a verbal, propositional revelation of fixed truth from God. Only by accepting rationally comprehensible information on God's authority can we hope to have a sound philosophy and a true religion.[49]

Clark not only defended the faith by tearing down other belief systems through use of the law of contradiction, but he (after presupposing the truth of Christianity) also was willing to confirm the truth of Christianity in two ways. First, Clark showed that it alone is self-consistent. And second, he appealed to its ability to provide man with meaning to life, moral values, and the genuine possibility of attaining true knowledge.[50] Since all other philosophies have failed to obtain knowledge, one must choose between skepticism and presupposing Christian revelation.[51]

Still, Clark seemed to revert back to fideism. This was due to his hyper-Calvinistic theology. He firmly believed that one really cannot convince another of the truth of Christianity, for God alone sovereignly bestows faith upon an individual.[52] When answering the question of why one person presupposes the Bible to be true and not the Muslim Koran, he simply replied that "God causes the one to believe."[53]

CLARK'S SOLUTION TO THE PROBLEM OF EVIL

In his writings, Gordon Clark attempted to answer the question, "How can the existence of God be harmonized with the existence of evil?"[54] If God is all-good, He would want to destroy evil. If God is all-powerful, He is able to destroy evil. But evil still exists. It seems that God cannot be both all-good and all-powerful. However, Christianity teaches that He is both. This is the problem of evil.[55]

Zoroastrianism attempts to resolve the problem by teaching that there are two gods. One is good while the other is evil. Neither of the two gods is infinite since they have both failed to destroy the opposing god. Plato's views also result in an unresolved dualism. In his thought, God is not the creator of all things. There exists eternal and chaotic space which the Demiurge cannot control.[56]

According to Clark, even Augustine's answer to the dilemma was inadequate. Clark stated that Augustine taught that evil is metaphysically unreal. It does not exist. Therefore, all that God created is good since evil is non-being.[57] (Whether or not Clark treated Augustine's view fairly will be discussed at a later point in this chapter.)

Clark pointed out that Augustine added to his response the doctrine of human free will. Though God is all-powerful, He has sovereignly chosen to give mankind free will. God allows man to make his own choices. Mankind has chosen evil. Therefore, all that God created is good. Evil can be blamed not on God, but on the abuse of free will by man.[58]

But Clark rejected this view of free will. Clark believed that the Bible does not teach that man is free to choose that which is right as opposed to that which is wrong. Clark stated that "free will is not only futile, but false. Certainly, if the Bible is the Word of God, free will is false; for the Bible consistently denies free will."[59]

Though Clark rejected the doctrine of free will, he believed man has free agency. "Free will means there is no determining factor operating on the will, not even God. Free will means that either of two incompatible actions are equally possible."[60] This Clark rejected. On the other hand,

"Free agency goes with the view that all choices are inevitable. The liberty that the Westminster Confession ascribes to the will is a liberty from compulsion, coaction, or force of inanimate objects; it is not a liberty from the power of God."[61] Clark argued that a man can still be responsible for his actions even without the freedom to do other than he has done. Clark stated that, "a man is responsible if he must answer for what he does . . . a person is responsible if he can be justly rewarded or punished for his deeds. This implies, of course, that he must be answerable to someone."[62]

Clark then asked the question, "Is it just then for God to punish a man for deeds that God Himself 'determined before to be done?'"[63] He answered in the affirmative. He stated that, "Whatever God does is just."[64] Man is responsible to God; but God is responsible to no one.

Clark openly admitted that his view makes God the cause of sin. For, in his thinking, "God is the sole ultimate cause of everything."[65] But, while God is the ultimate cause of sin, He is not the author of sin. The author is the immediate cause of an action. Man is the immediate cause of his sin. But he was not free to do otherwise. For God is the ultimate cause of sin.[66]

Clark stated that, "God's causing a man to sin is not sin. There is no law, superior to God, which forbids him to decree sinful acts. Sin presupposes a law, for sin is lawlessness."[67] Clark explained that "God is above law" because "the laws that God imposes on men do not apply to the divine nature."[68]

Clark stated:

> Man is responsible because God calls him to account; man is responsible because the supreme power can punish him for disobedience. God, on the contrary, cannot be responsible for the plain reason that there is no power superior to

him; no greater being can hold him accountable; no one can punish him; there is no one to whom God is responsible; there are no laws which he could disobey.

The sinner therefore, and not God, is responsible; the sinner alone is the author of sin. Man has no free will, for salvation is purely of grace; and God is sovereign.[69]

This was Clark's proposed solution to the problem of evil. God is in fact the ultimate cause of sin. But He is not evil, for He committed no sin. And He is not responsible for sin, for there is no one to whom He is responsible. God is just, for whatever He does is just. Therefore, the creature has no right to stand in judgment over his Creator.

STRENGTHS OF CLARK'S PRESUPPOSITIONALISM

Gordon Clark, as this study shows, was a very original thinker. Even if one disagrees with much of what he has written, he has made a tremendous contribution to Christian thought that should not be overlooked. There are several strengths which are evident in the thought of Gordon Clark.

His rejection of pure rationalism. Clark is absolutely correct when he points out the major deficiency of rationalism. That is, rationalism cannot even get started until certain unproven assumptions are made. Reason cannot prove everything. This would result in an infinite regress, and nothing would be proven. First principles must be presupposed. They are not logically necessary (they cannot be proven with rational certainty).

His rejection of pure empiricism. Clark is right when he points out problems with extreme empiricism. Sense data and the facts of history do not come with their own built-in interpretations. They must be interpreted within the context of a person's world view. Empirical data alone cannot give us rational conclusions.

His rejection of irrationalism. Clark should be commended for his lack of patience for irrationalism. Once a person denies the law of contradiction, then the opposite of whatever that person teaches can be equally true with those teachings. But all human thought and communication comes to a halt if one allows such an absurd premise. A person who holds to irrationalism cannot even express his view without assuming the truth of the law of contradiction.

His knowledge of the history of philosophical thought. Rarely does one read the works of a Christian author who has the insights that Clark had. His knowledge of the thought of the great philosophical minds of the past should encourage all Christians to be more diligent in their own studies. Gordon Clark was a man who had something to say because he was a man who lived a disciplined life of study. Even if one disagrees with the thrust of Clark's thought, one must never dismiss the insights he shared with others concerning the history of philosophy.

His recognition of the fact that all people have hidden presuppositions. Too often Christians pretend that they have no biases whatsoever, but this is not the case. Every person, believer and nonbeliever alike, has presuppositions that are often hidden. Clark was right in his view that apologetics is more accurately the seeking of confirmation for our presuppositions than it is the unbiased search for truth.

His use of the law of noncontradiction. Clark was justified in his usage of the law of noncontradiction. If two opposite concepts can both be true at the same time and in the same sense, then all knowledge and communication become impossible. Any world view that either is a contradiction or generates contradictions is not worth believing.

He is very consistent in his Calvinism. Too often Christians claim to be Calvinists but actually deny or redefine several of the five main points of Calvinism. Clark is not only a strong defender of all five points, but he also consistently holds to the implications of these points. His rejection of human free will and his view of God as the ultimate cause of evil are unpopular concepts, even among Calvinists. Clark is to be credited with having the courage to believe that which is consistent with his system of thought.

He is right to seek confirmation for his Christian pre-suppositions. Many presuppositionalists are content in merely assuming the truth of Christianity. But Clark realizes that, after pre-supposing biblical truth, one must still seek justification for this assumption. Clark does this by showing that Christianity does what all secular philosophies have failed to do. They failed to give meaning to life, justify moral values, and find truth.

He is right that man must choose. Clark recognizes that since all secular philosophies have failed to justify their truth claims, man must make a choice. A person can choose to continue to live with contradictory views. Or a person can choose skepticism and suspend all judgment (except his judgment to be skeptical). Clark even remarks that, for some, suicide is their choice.[70] But Clark pleads with his readers to choose Christianity. If secular philosophies have failed to find truth and give meaning to life, then why not choose Christianity? Whatever the case, man must choose.

THE WEAKNESSES OF CLARK'S PRESUPPOSITIONALISM

His denial of the basic reliability of sense perception. Though Clark is correct when he states that concepts such as moral values, causality, time, and space cannot be derived from sense data alone, he goes too far when he speaks of the "futility of sensation."[71] With Clark's distrust for sense experience, how can he presuppose the truth of the Bible? For he must first use his sense of sight to read the Bible to find out what it is he is going to presuppose. In fact, the Bible itself seems to teach the basic reliability of sense perception. The Mosaic Law places great emphasis on eyewitness testimony, and the eyewitness accounts of Christ's post-resurrection appearances are presented as evidence for the truth of Christ's claims.

His denial of Thomistic first principles. While refuting rationalism, Clark stated that it needed first principles. For justification must stop somewhere. He pointed out that since first principles could not be proven through reason alone, rationalism fails to find truth without appealing to something other than reason. The first principles are not logically necessary. In this he is correct. However, Clark accepts the law of contradiction (what Thomists call the law of noncontradiction), though he says it is not logically necessary. He points out that if we do not accept this law, all knowledge and communication would cease. However, this is the same type of argument that Aquinas (and Aristotle long before him) used for his remaining first principles. Besides the principle of noncontradiction, Aquinas utilized the principles of identity, excluded middle, causality, and finality.[72] Aristotle and Aquinas argued that these principles "cannot actually be denied without absurdity."[73] In other words, they are actually undeniable (though not logically necessary). But this is very similar to what Clark claims for one of his first principles, the law of contradiction. If Clark is justified in using this principle, then the other Thomistic first principles of knowledge may likewise be justified. If one accepts the principle of causality (every effect has an adequate cause), then one can reason from the effect (the finite world) to its cause (the infinite Creator). This would deal Clark's entire system a lethal blow since it would justify the use of traditional arguments for God's existence. This would eliminate presuppositional apologetics as the only way for a Christian to defend his faith.

His downplaying of historical evidences for the Christian Faith. Clark rightly criticized deriving knowledge from sense data alone. Because of this, he minimized historical evidences. For facts of history, like sense data, do not come with their own built-in interpretations. However, if one accepts Thomistic first principles (because they are actually undeniable), then one can attempt to make sense of the facts of history. If a man claimed to be God and rose from the dead to prove His claim true, then one is not justified in explaining this resurrection in purely naturalistic terms. For every event must have an adequate cause. And no naturalistic explanation has succeeded to account for the resurrection.[74] Only a supernatural cause is sufficient in this case.

He gives no credit to probability arguments. Clark points out that other systems of philosophy do not have a starting point based on certainty. They must presuppose their first principles. However, Clark's own first principles are also not based on certainty; they too must be presupposed. It seems that Clark is judging his own philosophical system in a more lenient fashion than he does other schools of thought. It is true that Clark finds confirmation for the Christian presupposition that is lacking in other presuppositions. Still, this is after the fact. And, as Clark admits, this confirmation itself only makes Christianity more probable than other views; it does not establish its certainty. It seems that more credit should be given to arguments for first principles based upon a high degree of probability. Why should an argument be rejected when its premises and conclusion are very probable, while opposing views are unlikely?

Other philosophers have settled for less than certainty but still have solid systems of thought. Some might argue from premises that they believe are "beyond all reasonable doubt." Norman Geisler, following in the tradition of Thomas Aquinas, uses the principle of "actual undeniability."[75] Some things cannot be denied without contradiction and therefore must be true. For instance, if I deny my existence I must first exist to make the denial. For nothing is nothing. Nothing cannot deny anything. Only an existent being can deny something. Therefore, it is actually undeniable that I exist.[76]

Charles Hodge (1797-1878) based his philosophical arguments on what he believed were "self-evident truths." Though these truths could be denied by others, their denial is "forced and temporary."

Once a philosopher finishes lecturing or debating, he returns to the real world and no longer denies self-evident truths such as his existence, the existence of others, and the reality of moral values.[77] He can deny moral values in the lecture hall, but once he is at home, he calls the police when he is robbed.

It seems then that Clark is mistaken. Christians can discover truths that are either "self-evident" or "actually undeniable." They can then dialogue with nonbelievers using these premises as common ground. Clark was wrong not to give proper due to first principles based upon a high degree of probability. This leaves the door open for traditional apologetics.

His attacks on traditional apologetics. Clark's attack on traditional apologetics is unfounded. This can be shown from his treatment of the Thomistic cosmological argument for God's existence. Aquinas argued that all existent beings which could possibly not exist need a cause or ground for their continuing in existence. In other words, all dependent existence must rely for its continued existence on a totally independent Being, a Being which is uncaused and self-existent.[78]

Clark comments that Aquinas has not ruled out the possibility of an infinite regress of dependent beings.[79] However, Clark is mistaken. For Aquinas is not arguing indefinitely into the past. He is arguing for the current existence of a totally independent Being. Aquinas is arguing for the cause of the continued and present existence of dependent beings, not just the cause for the beginning of their existence.[80] Aquinas is pointing out that if one takes away the independent Being, then there is nothing to sustain the existence of all dependent beings. Every dependent being relies directly on the independent Being for preserving it in existence. The causality is simultaneous, just as a person's face simultaneously causes the existence of its reflection in a mirror. At the exact moment the person moves his face, the reflection is gone.

Clark raises another objection against the Thomistic cosmological argument. He states that even if the argument is valid, it would not prove the existence of the God of the Bible. Clark seems to imply that unless we prove every attribute of God, then it is not the identical God.[81] However, if Aquinas proves the existence of the Uncaused Cause of all else that exists, how could this possibly not be the God of the Bible? If Clark can refer to God as "Truth" and "Logic" and still be talking about the Triune God of the Bible, then Aquinas can identify God with the "Unmoved Mover."

Finally, Clark accuses Aquinas of using the word "exist" with two completely different meanings.[82] When Aquinas speaks of God, he speaks of God existing infinitely. But when he speaks of man, he speaks of man existing finitely. God is existence; man merely has existence. Though Clark's critique may seem valid, it is not. Aquinas would define existence as "that which is" whether it referred to God or man. True, Aquinas would apply the term "existence" to God infinitely, but to man only finitely. Still, the fact remains that whether Aquinas speaks of God or man, the meaning of existence remains the same.

Apparently, Clark misunderstands Aquinas' view of analogical language. Aquinas taught that we cannot have univocal (totally the same) knowledge of God. Still, our knowledge of God is not equivocal (totally different) since that would be no knowledge at all. Instead, according to Aquinas, our knowledge of God is analogical (similar). By this Aquinas did not mean that the concepts used of God and man have similar meanings. He meant that they have identical meanings, but that they must be applied only in a similar way. All limitations must be removed from a concept before it is applied to God. However, the concept itself continues to have the same meaning throughout.[83]

Not only did Clark express distaste for the cosmological argument for God's existence, he also disliked the teleological argument (the argument from design).[84] He accepted Hume's criticism of this argument. Hume concluded that it proved the existence only of a finite god or gods, and that this god or gods may be evil (due to the evil in the world). However, if one argues for the existence of one infinite God through the cosmological argument, and then finishes the argument with the teleological premises, the argument from design will add the attribute of intelligence to the Uncaused Cause. The problem of evil could also be dealt with as a separate issue. In short, Clark's attempt to destroy traditional apologetics has failed.

His failure to refute the Islamic Faith. After destroying secular philosophy through the use of the law of contradiction, Clark does not apply this law to Islam. Instead, he merely states that God causes some to accept the Bible when answering the question, "Why does one man accept the Koran and another the Bible?"[85] Apparently, after all is said and done, Clark's system relies on God alone to cause the person to believe. One wonders why Clark went to such trouble to refute secular philosophies. Could not the same response be given to them?

His misrepresentation of Augustine and Aquinas. While dealing with the problem of evil, Clark accused Augustine of denying the reality of evil. He stated that

Augustine taught that "all existing things are good" and that "evil therefore does not exist—it is metaphysically unreal."[86] Clark represented Augustine as reasoning that since evil does not exist, God cannot be the cause of evil.[87] In this way, Clark makes it sound as if Augustine is in agreement with the Christian Science view of evil as an illusion. Clark is misrepresenting Augustine on this point.

Augustine did teach that God created everything that exists and that all that God created is good. However, evil is a perversion of that good brought about by the free choices of rational beings (fallen angels and men). Evil is a privation. It is a lack of a good that should be there.[88] An illustration of this would be rust. God did not create rust. Still it exists, but only as a corruption of something that God created (metal). Therefore, evil is real, but it must exist in some good thing that God created. All that God created is good. God did not create evil. He created the possibility of evil (free will). Fallen rational beings actualized evil by abusing a good thing (free will) God gave them.

Clark also misrepresents Aquinas by downplaying Aquinas' emphasis on the active mind. It is true that Aquinas believed all knowledge comes through sense experience, but he also taught that God created man's mind with the innate ability to draw rational conclusions from sense data. Aquinas spoke of both the active mind (this innate ability to arrive at universals from particulars) and the receptive mind (the aspect of the mind which receives data from sense experience). Clark focuses on Aquinas' doctrine of the receptive mind, while de-emphasizing Aquinas' teaching about the active mind (also called the agent intellect).[89]

His proposed solution to the problem of evil. Clark's answer to the problem of evil is inadequate. He stated that God is not responsible for evil simply because there is no one above Him to whom He is responsible. Since Clark denied human free will (man could not choose to do otherwise),

Clark made God the ultimate cause of evil.

The Augustinian approach, in the opinion of many Christian philosophers, is to be preferred. Augustine held that God gave man the freedom to disobey His commands. Therefore, God permitted sin; it was not part of His perfect will for man. A free will theodicy (attempting to propose a reason why God permitted evil) or a free will defense (attempting to merely show that it is not impossible for an all-good and all-powerful God to coexist with evil) is a much more plausible solution to the problem of evil than the solution Clark proposed.[90] Of course, since Clark denied genuine free will, these options were not open to him.

He does not allow for the use of secular material during evangelism. Clark states, "in evangelistic work there can be no appeal to secular, non-Christian material."[91] However, this is exactly what the apostle Paul did on Mars Hill. When speaking to Stoic and Epicurean philosophers, he quoted from the writings of two ancient Greek poets to find common ground with his hearers (Acts 17:16-34). If one must choose between the evangelistic approach of Gordon Clark and that of the apostle Paul, then one should choose Paul.

No Christian can show that every non-Christian system of thought is inconsistent. Clark claims that since every non-Christian philosophy has failed, people should presuppose the truth of the Christian world view. However, it is impossible for Clark, or any other person, to thoroughly examine every non-Christian system of thought.[92] Even if it were possible for Clark to expose the contradictions in every non-Christian world view today, there is no guarantee that a totally consistent non-Christian world view will not be produced in the future.[93]

CONCLUSION

Clark's presuppositional approach to apologetics, with minor adaptions, is a worthy apologetic. Uncovering contradictions in non-Christian belief systems is a necessary component in one's defense of the faith. However, Clark's presuppositional approach is not the only method Christians can use when defending the faith. Although Clark successfully demolishes several secular philosophies, traditional apologetics survives his assault.

ENDNOTES

[1] Gordon H. Clark, *Clark Speaks From the Grave* (Jefferson: The Trinity Foundation, 1986), 2.

[2] Gordon H. Clark, *Religion, Reason and Revelation* (Jefferson: The Trinity Foundation, 1986), 35.

[3] Ibid., 37.

[4] Clark, *Clark Speaks From the Grave*, 54.

[5] Ibid., 55.

[6] Ibid., 57.

[7] Geisler, *Apologetics*, 37.

[8] Gordon H. Clark, *Thales to Dewey* (Jefferson: The Trinity Foundation, 1989), 534.

[9] Geisler and Feinberg, 431.

[10] Gordon H. Clark, *Three Types of Religious Philosophy* (Jefferson: The Trinity Foundation, 1989), 60-61.

[11] Geisler, *Thomas Aquinas*, 86.

[12] Ibid.

[13] Clark, *Three Types of Religious Philosophy*, 64-70.

[14] Ibid., 71,76-78.

[15] Ibid., 91.

[16] Ibid., 27.

[17] Ibid., 28-29.

[18] Ibid., 31.

[19] Ibid., 32.

[20] Ibid., 33-35.

[21] Clark, Religion, *Reason and Revelation,* 50-51.

[22] Clark, *Three Types of Religious Philosophy,* 35.

[23] Clark, *Thales to Dewey,* 332.

[24] Clark, *Religion, Reason and Revelation,* 53.

[25] Clark, *Three Types of Religious Philosophy,* 56.

[26] Ibid., 117-118.

[27] Ibid., 120.

[28] Ibid., 93.

[29] Clark, *Religion, Reason and Revelation,* 62.

[30] Gordon H. Clark, *A Christian View of Men and Things* (Jefferson: The Trinity Foundation, 1991), 315-316.

[31] Clark, *Religion, Reason and Revelation,* 63-68.

[32] Ibid., 98.

[33] Clark, *Three Types of Religious Philosophy,* 101-105.

[34] Ibid., 114.

[35] Clark, *Thales to Dewey,* 534.

[36] Clark, *Three Types of Religious Philosophy,* 116.

[37] Ibid., 118.

[38] Ibid., 51-52.

[39] Ibid., 70-91.

[40] Ibid., 118-119.

[41] Clark, *A Christian View of Men and Things,* 324.

[42] Ibid.

[43] Ibid.

[44] Ibid., 315-316.

[45] Ibid., 316.

[46] Clark, *Three Types of Religious Philosophy,* 140-142.

[47] Sproul, Gerstner, and Lindsley, 76.

[48] Ibid.

[49] Clark, *Religion, Reason and Revelation,* 87.

[50] Clark, *A Christian View of Men and Things,* 324.

[51] Clark, *Religion, Reason and Revelation,* 109-110.

[52] Clark, *Three Types of Religious Philosophy,* 138.

[53] Ibid., 139.

[54] Clark, *Religion, Reason and Revelation,* 195.

[55] Ibid.

[56] Ibid., 195-196.

[57] Ibid., 196.

[58] Ibid., 199.

[59] Ibid., 206.

[60] Ibid., 227.

[61] Ibid.

[62] Ibid., 231.

[63] Ibid.

[64] Ibid., 232-233.

[65] Ibid., 237-238.

[66] Ibid., 237-239.

[67] Ibid., 239-240.

[68] Ibid., 240.

[69] Ibid., 241.

[70] Clark, *Thales to Dewey,* 534.

[71] Clark, *Three Types of Religious Philosophy,* 91.

[72] Geisler, *Thomas Aquinas,* 72-74.

[73] Ibid., 78-79.

[74] Habermas, 26-33.

[75] Geisler, *Apologetics,* 143.

[76] Ibid., 143-144.

[77] Charles Hodge, *Systematic Theology* (Grand Rapids: Eerdmans Publishing Company, 1989), vol. 1, 210.

[78] Thomas Aquinas, *Summa Theologiae,* 1a. 2,3.

[79] Clark, Religion, *Reason and Revelation,* 36-37.

[80] Craig, *Apologetics,* 63-65.

[81] Clark, *Religion, Reason and Revelation,* 37-38.

[82] Ibid., 38-39.

[83] Geisler, *Thomas Aquinas,* 40.

[84] Clark, *Three Types of Religious Philosophy,* 64-70.

[85] Ibid., 139.

[86] Clark, *Religion, Reason and Revelation,* 196.

[87] Ibid.

[88] Augustine, *The City of God,* 22.1.

[89] Geisler, *Thomas Aquinas,* 86.

[90] Alvin C. Plantinga, *God, Freedom, and Evil* (Grand Rapids: Eerdmans Publishing Company, 1974), 28-31.

[91] Clark, *Three Types of Religious Philosophy,* 139.

[92] Gordon R. Lewis, 119.

[93] Ibid., 119-120.

CORNELIUS VAN TIL'S TRANSCENDENTAL PRESUPPOSITIONALISM

G ordon Clark was not alone in his use of presuppositional apologetics. Another Calvinist scholar named Cornelius Van Til (1895-1987) also used this methodology. Despite the fact that both thinkers were presuppositionalists, they differed on many key points. Clark's presuppositionalism could be called dogmatic presuppositionalism,[1] whereas Van Til utilized what could be called transcendental presuppositionalism.[2] Still, their thought systems had much in common.

REJECTION OF TRADITIONAL APOLOGETICS

Like Clark, Van Til was opposed to traditional methods of apologetics. Van Til taught that because of man's Fall in the garden "every one of fallen man's functions operates wrongly."[3] Van Til stated that "on account of sin man is blind with respect to truth wherever truth appears."[4] Van Til taught that without the correct view about God, man cannot have the correct view of himself and the world.[5]

According to Van Til, the unsaved man is biased against God; he presupposes his own autonomy.[6] The unsaved man believes he can start with himself and find truth without aid from God. There is therefore no neutral ground between believers and nonbelievers.[7]

The nonbeliever presupposes human autonomy; the believer presupposes the existence of God.

However, there is common ground: all mankind must live within God's universe.[8] All men live in the real world of reason and moral values. Because of this common ground, believers can reason with nonbelievers. Still, with the absence of neutral ground, traditional apologetics cannot even get started. People are not unbiased observers who allow the facts to determine their world view. Instead, people interpret the facts by their preconceived world view (their presuppositions or biases).[9] Therefore, all apologetics must be by way of presupposition.[10]

Van Til disagrees with Roman Catholicism for declaring the autonomy of human reason. Roman Catholicism "ascribes ultimacy or self-sufficiency to the mind of man."[11] When Arminians, Evangelicals, and "less consistent" Calvinists defend the faith, they take the side of the Roman Church by assuming the mind of the unsaved man can of itself rise to a proper understanding of the Triune God.[12] Only a consistent Calvinistic position rightly denies the nonbeliever the ability to reason correctly (without faulty biases).

Van Til adds that traditional apologetics would never prove the existence of the Triune God of the Bible. Instead, traditional apologetics only proves the existence of a finite god.[13] Van Til states that Roman Catholicism would never desire to prove the existence of an infinite God who controls whatever comes to pass. The Roman Church, according to Van Til, wants to protect man's self-sufficiency.[14]

Van Til believed the root of the problem is found in

the fact that all nonbelievers suppress their knowledge of the true God (Romans 1:18-22). Concerning the unsaved man, Van Til states that "deep down in his mind every man knows that he is a creature of God and responsible to God. Every man, at bottom, knows that he is a covenant-breaker. But every man acts as though this were not so."[15] By using traditional apologetics, believers mistakenly assume that the unsaved man honestly needs proof that the God of the Bible exists. Instead, Christians should directly confront the nonbeliever by proclaiming the gospel message from the start.[16]

According to Van Til, traditional arguments are also misguided in that they use inductive arguments for Christianity. Inductive arguments are probabilistic; they do not prove their conclusions with certainty. Therefore, traditional arguments give nonbelievers an excuse for rejecting the truth of Christianity, for if Christianity is only probably true, then it is also possibly false. Van Til believed that what was needed was not a probabilistic argument for Christianity, but an argument that proved the impossibility of the contrary. Van Til believed that his transcendental argument alone proved Christianity to be true with certainty.[17]

The traditional arguments for God's existence are therefore useless. The nonbeliever must be confronted with the gospel. Only in this direct approach will the believer find a point of contact with the nonbeliever. It should not be assumed that the nonbeliever is an honest, neutral seeker of truth.[18]

REASONING BY PRESUPPOSITION

After rejecting traditional apologetics, Van Til unveils his own method of defending the faith. He states that "a truly Protestant apologetic must therefore make its beginning from the presupposition that the Triune God . . . speaks to him with absolute authority in Scripture."[19] Now that believers stand on Christian foundations, they can see "the futility of reasoning on non-Christian foundations . . ."[20] Thus, rather than argue to the existence of the Triune God who has spoken to man through His Word, apologists must presuppose His existence.

Van Til sees no middle ground at this point. Two opposing presuppositions are competing for a person's allegiance. The nonbeliever presupposes that he himself is the final or ultimate reference point in all human thought, but the believer rightly presupposes the final or ultimate reference point in human thought to be the Triune God who speaks to man through His infallible Word.[21] There is no neutral ground here.

If humans were really products of chance as the nonbeliever assumes is the case, then there would be no possibility of knowing the world, ourselves, or anything else.[22] But human thought and knowledge is possible because man is who the Bible declares him to be, a being created by God.[23]

Van Til does engage in refuting the beliefs of others. For the sake of argument, believers may "place themselves with the unbeliever on his presupposition" in order to expose the contradictions which the nonbeliever holds.[24] However, even the law of noncontradiction is not presupposed by the Christian. It is only borrowed from the nonbeliever's system of thought and used by the Christian to show the internal inconsistencies of the anti-Christian thought.

In Van Til's apologetic system, only the "Triune God revealed in Scripture" is presupposed.[25] Not even nature or the laws of logic are presupposed. For man to start with himself rather than with God would be to deny his utter dependence on God. One cannot argue for Christianity. Instead, the validity of the gospel must be presupposed. However, Van Til will allow believers to utilize the presuppositions of nonbelievers in order to refute their views.

CIRCULAR REASONING

Cornelius Van Til stated that "all reasoning is, in the nature of the case, circular reasoning."[26] By this he meant that "the starting-point, the method, and the conclusion are always involved in one another."[27] In other words, when attempting to prove something, a person must first assume the conclusion to be true before proving it to be true. Van Til was claiming that every argument contains its conclusion in its initial premise.

Philosophers refer to circular reasoning as "begging the question." It has long been considered an informal fallacy by logicians. To assume what you are attempting to prove has historically been considered to be an illegitimate form of argumentation. Most believers and nonbelievers agree on this point.

It is interesting that Van Til chooses to refer to "all reasoning" as circular. The point he is stressing is that we argue from our presuppositions, not to them.[28] Apart from regeneration by the Holy Spirit, a person will not presuppose the truth of Christianity.[29] Here, Van Til's Calvinism is evident.

PARADOX

Van Til does not believe that the law of contradiction can be found in God's being.[30] Whereas Gordon Clark viewed this law as an expression of God's very being, Van Til considers this law a human limitation that does not apply to God. He believed that Clark, and those who agree with him, make God subject to a human law. Van Til warns that the rational man will allow his reason to sit in judgment over God's Word. He will not allow the Bible to rule his life.[31]

Van Til goes so far as to speak of God's Word as seemingly contradicting itself. Though he states that God does not actually contradict Himself, he adds that God's communication to man often appears contradictory to finite human minds.[32] But, Van Til cannot have it both ways. Either God cannot contradict Himself and the law of contradiction flows from His nature, or God can contradict Himself and the law is merely a human limitation.

If by paradox Van Til simply means an apparent contradiction, then even Clark would agree with his premise. Therefore, any criticism that Van Til made of Clark on this point would also apply to Van Til himself. However, if his usage of the term paradox does mean an actual contradiction, then nothing could be known of God.

For God could both love mankind and not love mankind at the same time and in the same sense. It seems that Van Til should have withdrawn his criticism of Clark in this area and admitted that the law of contradiction flows naturally from God's being.

THE TRANSCENDENTAL ARGUMENT

Though Van Til rejected traditional apologetics, he was willing to do more than refute the nonbeliever's world view. Van Til was willing to use one argument for the truth of Christianity. He believed it to be the only valid argument for the true God. He called this argument the transcendental argument.

The transcendental argument attempts to uncover the hidden presuppositions of the nonbeliever. These hidden presuppositions are the necessary preconditions for human thought.[33] Van Til argued that all human thought and moral judgments would be impossible if the Christian God did not exist. Van Til claimed that if God did not exist, then man would know nothing. Even for man to be conscious of his own existence presupposes a consciousness of God's existence. When a nonbeliever argues against God's existence, he must first presuppose God's existence just to argue at all.[34]

For the sake of argument, a believer can place himself within the unbeliever's world view to show that the unbeliever has to presuppose the truth of Christianity just to raise an objection against Christianity.[35] Only Christianity justifies man's ability to reason. Only Christianity gives meaning to life. All other world views lead to irrationality and chaos.[36] In fact, scientific induction makes no

sense in a universe without God, for only the Christian God guarantees the uniformity and order of nature necessary for scientists to argue from the particulars of nature to general conclusions about the world in which he lives.[37]

COMPARISON WITH GORDON CLARK

When comparing the thought of Cornelius Van Til with that of Gordon Clark, one finds several points of agreement as well as several areas of disagreement. First, some points of agreement between these two men will be examined.

Both were serious and consistent Calvinists. Because they both believed that no one could freely choose Christ apart from the Holy Spirit's regenerating work, direct attempts to persuade nonbelievers were thought to be counterproductive.

Both agreed that the gospel should be presupposed and not argued for. Van Til and Clark felt that to defend the truth of the gospel was to deny the Calvinist doctrine of the total depravity of man. They both believed that man's reason was damaged due to the Fall and that direct argumentation for the truth of Christianity would be useless. Still, both were willing to refute the beliefs of the nonbeliever and provide indirect confirmation for the truth of Christianity.

Both agreed that secular philosophy was a complete failure. Clark taught that all non-Christian philosophy eventually reduced to skepticism. Van Til believed that secular philosophy was futile since human reason was fallen. In his view, without presupposing the God of the Bible, no knowledge was attainable. However, Van Til believed that even nonbelievers presuppose God's existence (though they suppress this truth) in order to find truth.

Both agreed that traditional apologetics is unbiblical and useless. Throughout their writings, Clark and Van Til belittled the traditional method of defending the faith. They believed that there was no neutral battle ground between the believer and nonbeliever where Christianity could be defended. The gospel was to be presupposed rather than defended. They saw no use for the classical arguments for God's existence or for traditional usage of historical evidences for the Christian Faith.

Besides these points of agreement between Clark and Van Til, there were areas of disagreement. The following examples will illustrate this.

They disagreed about circular reasoning. Van Til believed that all reasoning is circular. The conclusion of one's arguments can always be found in one's premises. However, Clark was more rationalistic in his thinking. He considered circular reasoning a logical fallacy. Because of this, Clark dogmatically presupposed his first principle (the existence of the God of the Bible) and then deduced his beliefs from this first principle.

They disagreed about the status and use of the law of contradiction. Clark believed that the law of contradiction flowed from God's nature. He taught that God is logic. Therefore, when he presupposed the Triune God who revealed Himself in the Bible, he also presupposed the law of contradiction. He would then use this law to destroy the belief systems of nonbelievers.

Van Til, however, believed this law to be a human limitation which Clark forced upon God. Van Til believed that Clark had subjected God to this law. Though Van Til would use this law to refute other belief systems, it was only because he chose to use the "enemy's own ammunition to defeat the enemy in battle." In fact, Clark's view of the law of noncontradiction is probably what caused the widest gap between the thought of these two men. Clark presupposed the law of noncontradiction when doing apologetics. Van Til refused to do so.

STRENGTHS OF VAN TIL'S SYSTEM

In the presuppositional apologetics of Cornelius Van Til there is much to be commended. The following examples will make this clear.

He stresses the sinfulness of man. Too often, defenders of the faith tend to de-emphasize the effects of the Fall on mankind. But this is not true of Van Til. If Van Til can be accused of any fault in this area, it would be overkill. For, due to his Calvinism, man is not free to accept Christ; regeneration precedes faith.

He stresses man's suppression of God's truth. Many apologists assume that the reason why nonbelievers do not come to Christ is merely an intellectual one. Van Til rightly shows that men willfully suppress whatever knowledge of the true God they have. Van Til is correct in his view that the problem is ultimately that of a moral choice rather than an intellectual one. God has proven his existence to all men through His visible creation (Romans 1:18-22). Therefore, man has no excuse for rejecting Him.

He stresses God's work in salvation. Even non-Calvinists should commend Van Til for his focus on God's work in salvation. Apart from God's grace, no man would be saved. Traditional apologists often imply that they can lead people to Christ through argumentation alone. More emphasis is needed on the inward persuasion of the Holy Spirit concerning those to whom apologists witness. God can use traditional argumentation. Still, it is God who does the saving.

The apologist can remove intellectual stumbling blocks to the faith, but only God can persuade one to turn to Christ.

He stresses the importance of faith over reason. Van Til emphasizes that one must believe in Christ to be saved. Without Christ, even the wisest man in the world will be eternally lost.

Though traditional apologists are right in that man can reason to the true faith (Van Til disagrees with this), once a person through reason finds the true faith, he must submit his reason to it.

He is willing to tear down the belief systems of those who oppose the gospel and use an indirect argument for Christianity. If it were not for this point, Van Til would probably be classified as a fideist. Though he rejects traditional apologetics (like the fideist), he is willing to refute non-Christian views and give one argument for his beliefs (unlike the fideist). Van Til's transcendental argument goes beyond refuting non-Christian world views; it presents positive evidence for the Christian faith. Still, it does so in an indirect manner, rather than in the direct fashion found in traditional apologetics.

WEAKNESSES OF VAN TIL'S SYSTEM

Despite the many good things that could be said about Van Til's apologetics, there are many weaknesses in his thought. A few of these weaknesses are mentioned below.

He denies that man has the ability to test revelation-claims. Given Van Til's system, there seems to be no way to decide whether the Bible or the Koran is the Word of God. Yet the Bible frequently commands us to test the spirits, the prophets, and the messages they proclaim (1 Jn 4:1; Deut 18:20-22; Mt 7:15-23; Gal 1:8-9).[38] Also, God provided ample evidence for His revelation-claims by performing miracles through His spokesmen and by raising Jesus from the dead (Jn 20:30-31; 1 Cor 15:3-8). It seems that God has given even fallen man the ability to test revelation-claims. Whether or not man uses this ability wisely is another question. Again, Van Til's Calvinism can be seen. For without regeneration by the Holy Spirit, no one will accept the Bible as God's Word.

His view that all reasoning is circular. It is true that much of Van Til's thought is circular. It is not true that all thought is circular. Even though all men have presuppositions, they can be tested just as scientific hypotheses are tested. One does not have to sneak one's presuppositions into the premises of one's arguments. Any argument that uses circular reasoning is fallacious, regardless of whether or not the conclusion is true.

His rejection of the law of noncontradiction being universally valid. Though Van Til claimed that he only used the law of noncontradiction for the sake of argument when he shared his faith with nonbelievers, he often criticized many of his colleagues for being inconsistent Calvinists.[39] Though Van Til implied that this law is a man-made principle, he diligently labored to keep his system free from contradictions. Van Til should have realized that there could be no thought or communication whatsoever without the law of contradiction. Even God cannot contradict Himself. And, since God is not subject to anything outside Himself, Clark was right to view this law as naturally flowing from God's being.

Van Til's transcendental argument is not the only valid argument for Christianity. Even John Frame, a former student of Van Til, saw problems with Van Til's transcendental argument.[40] Although Frame recognized the worth of this argument for apologetics, he did not believe it was the only valid argument for Christianity.

First, Frame doubts that the transcendental argument could be persuasive without "the help of subsidiary arguments of a more traditional kind."[41] Second, Frame thinks Van Til was wrong in his assertion that the traditional arguments proved something less than the God of the Bible.[42] Third, Frame believes that some traditional arguments often work despite the fact that the traditional apologist might wrongly assume that their arguments do not themselves presuppose a Christian world view.[43] Fourth, Frame doubts that the whole of the Christian faith can be established by a single argument which stands alone.[44] Fifth, if Van Til is right in his claim that the apologist must prove the whole biblical doctrine of God rather than just one or a few of His attributes, then the transcendental argument also fails. For the God of the Bible is more than the source of meaning, morality, and rationality. Even the transcendental argument must be supplemented by other arguments.[45] And, sixth, Frame believes that any argument (including the transcendental argument) can be rejected. Hence, further argumentation may be needed to defend the original argument.[46] Therefore, though the transcendental argument of Van Til may be a good argument for the God of the Bible, it is not the only good argument for the God of the Bible. The traditional arguments (cosmological, teleological, moral) for God's existence may also be used by the apologist.

His rejection of traditional apologetics. Finally, Van Til was wrong to reject traditional apologetics. The Bible commands believers to defend the faith (1 Peter 3:15; Colossians 4:5-6). The apostles used historical evidences to lead others to Christ (1 Corinthians 15:3-8). Even Van Til admits that man suppresses the truth that God has given him in nature (Romans 1:18-22). If this is the case, then why shouldn't apologists use traditional arguments to attempt to dislodge these truths from the nonbelievers' subconscious mind? As the last chapter showed, traditional apologetics is on much more solid ground than the presuppositional apologetics of either Van Til or Clark would admit.

ENDNOTES

[1] Gordon H. Clark, *Three Types of Religious Philosophy,* 115-142.

[2] John M. Frame, *Apologetics to the Glory of God* (Phillipsburg: Presbyterian and Reformed Publishing, 1994), 69-75.

[3] Cornelius Van Til, *Christian Apologetics* (Phillipsburg: Presbyterian and Reformed Publishing Co., 1976), 43.

[4] Ibid., 42.

[5] Cornelius Van Til, *The Defense of the Faith* (Phillipsburg: Presbyterian and Reformed Publishing Co., 1967), 73.

[6] Ibid., 34.

[7] Ibid., 298.

[8] Ibid.

[9] Gordon R. Lewis, 128.

[10] Van Til, *Defense of the Faith,* 34, 99-105, 179-180, 195, 197.

[11] Ibid., 90.

[12] Ibid., 78-79.

[13] Ibid., 77.

[14] Ibid., 78.

[15] Ibid., 92, 94, 231.

[16] Ibid., 94.

[17] Ibid., 103.

[18] Ibid., 94.

[19] Ibid., 99-105, 179-180, 195, 197.

[20] Ibid., 180.

[21] Ibid.

[22] Ibid.

[23] Ibid.

[24] Ibid.

[25] Gordon R. Lewis, 131.

[26] Van Til, *The Defense of the Faith,* 101.

[27] Ibid.

[28] Ibid.

[29] Ibid., 299.

[30] Ibid., 298.

[31] Lewis, 133.

[32] Ibid.

[33] Van Til, *The Defense of the Faith,* 60, 150, 180, 298.

[34] Frame, 69-75.

[35] Van Til, *The Defense of the Faith,* 180.

[36] Ibid.

[37] Ibid.

[38] Gordon R. Lewis, 144.

[39] Ibid., 146.

[40] Frame, 69-75.

[41] Ibid., 71.

[42] Ibid.

[43] Ibid., 71-72.

[44] Ibid., 72.

[45] Ibid., 73.

[46] Ibid.

THE APOLOGETIC METHODOLOGY OF BLAISE PASCAL

B laise Pascal (1623-1662) was a French mathematician and scientist who is famous for his work dealing with the pressure of liquids and the theory of probability. He also designed a calculating machine, and, at the age of 16, wrote a book on Geometry which caught the attention of the great mathematician, Rene Descartes.[1]

Pascal was a devout Roman Catholic who had a vibrant faith in Jesus Christ.[2] Towards the end of his life, Pascal began to write and gather notes for a book on Christian apologetics. Unfortunately, Pascal died before he completed the project. A few years after his death the notes were published in a book entitled Pensees, which means "thoughts."[3]

Since Pascal did not himself complete his task on the Pensees, readers must study Pascal's ideas and attempt to organize them in as coherent a fashion as possible. Recent advancements have been made in this area by Tom Morris[4] of Notre Dame and Peter Kreeft[5] of Boston College.

In this chapter, I will attempt to construct a basic outline of the apologetic methodology of Blaise Pascal. I will also attempt to show the contemporary relevance of the Pascalian method.

PASCAL'S VIEW OF REASON

Pascal was opposed to the use of traditional proofs for God's existence. He wrote:

> The metaphysical proofs for the existence of God are so remote from human reasoning and so involved that they make little impact, and, even if they did help some people, it would only be for the moment during which they watched the demonstration, because an hour later they would be afraid they had made a mistake. (190)[6]

> And this is why I shall not undertake here to prove by reasons from nature either the existence of God, or the Trinity or the immortality of the soul, or anything of that kind: not just because I should not feel competent to find in nature arguments which would convince hardened atheists, but also because such knowledge, without Christ, is useless and sterile. Even if someone were convinced that the proportions between numbers are immaterial, eternal truths, depending on a first truth in which they subsist, called God, I should not consider that he made much progress towards his salvation. The Christian's God does not consist merely of a God who is the author of mathematical truths and the order of the elements. That is the portion of the heathen and Epicureans. (449)

Pascal believed that even if these arguments were valid, few would reason well enough to be persuaded by them. And, even if the arguments persuaded someone, that person would still not be saved. Pascal was concerned with leading people to Christ, not merely to monotheism (the belief in the existence of one God). Therefore, he believed the traditional arguments for God's existence were counterproductive.

Pascal was also opposed to the pure rationalism of Descartes. Pascal realized that there were more ways to find truth than through reason alone. Man could also find truth through his heart. By the heart, Pascal meant what we intuitively know as opposed to what we know through deductive reasoning.[7] We perceive and believe in God with our hearts. We will with our hearts.[8] We know first principles through the heart. Pascal not only recognized other ways of knowing besides reason, but he saw that man's reason is often influenced by other factors. Man is not always true to his reason. Pascal's view of reason can be seen in the following quotes:

> We know the truth not only through our reason but also through our heart. It is through the latter that we know first principles, and reason, which has nothing to do with it, tries in vain to refute them. The skeptics have no other object than that, and they work at it to no purpose. We know that we are not dreaming, but, however unable we may be to prove it rationally, our inability proves nothing but the weakness of our reason, and not the uncertainty of all our knowledge, as they maintain. For knowledge of first principles, like space, time, motion, number, is as solid as any derived through reason, and it is on such knowledge, coming from the heart and instinct, that reason has to depend

and base all its argument. . . It is just as pointless and absurd for reason to demand proof of first principles from the heart before agreeing to accept them as it would be absurd for the heart to demand an intuition of all the propositions demonstrated by reason before agreeing to accept them. Our inability must therefore serve only to humble reason, which would like to be judge of everything, but not to confute our certainty. As if reason were the only way we could learn! (110)

The mind of this supreme judge of the world. . . Do not be surprised if his reasoning is not too sound at the moment, there is a fly buzzing round his ears; this is enough to render him incapable of giving good advice. (48)

Would you not say that this magistrate, whose venerable age commands universal respect, is ruled by pure, sublime reason, and judges things as they really are, without paying heed to the trivial circumstances which offend only the imagination of the weaker men? See him go to hear a sermon . . . If, when the preacher appears, it turns out that nature has given him a hoarse voice and an odd sort of face, that his barber has shaved him badly and he happens not to be too clean either, then, whatever great truths he may announce, I wager that our senator will not be able to keep a straight face. . . Anyone who chose to follow reason alone would have proved himself a fool. . . Reason never wholly overcomes imagination, while the contrary is quite common. (44)

Be humble, impotent reason! Be silent, feeble

nature! Learn that man infinitely transcends man, hear from your master your true condition, which is unknown to you. Listen to God. (131)

Descartes. . . we do not think that the whole of philosophy would be worth an hour's effort. (84)

The heart has its reasons of which reason knows nothing. (423)
It is the heart which perceives God and not the reason. That is what faith is: God perceived by the heart, not by the reason. (424)

It is important to note that Pascal is not an irrationalist. He recognizes that reason has its place; still, he reminds us that there are other ways of finding truth besides reason:

Two excesses: to exclude reason, to admit nothing but reason. (183)

Reason's last step is the recognition that there are an infinite number of things beyond it. It is merely feeble if it does not go as far as to realize that. If natural things are beyond it, what are we to say about supernatural things? (188)

If we submit everything to reason our religion will be left with nothing mysterious or supernatural. (173)

It is apparent that Pascal is not a fideist. He believed there was a place for reason in religious discussions. Still, he was not a pure rationalist. He differed from Descartes in that he did not believe that man could find all truth through reason alone; he did not believe man could deduce everything from from one point of rational certainty. Pascal respected the role of reason in knowing truth; but, he also recognized that reason has its limits.[9]

Pascal was willing, as we shall see, to use reason to defend the Christian Faith. Still, he recognized man to be more than a thinking machine. Man comes complete with prejudices, emotions, a will, and a vivid imagination. The whole man must be evangelized, not just his mind. According to Peter Kreeft, "Like Augustine, Pascal knows that the heart is deeper than the head, but like Augustine he does not cut off his own head, or so soften it up with relativism and subjectivism and 'open-mindedness' that his brains fall out."[10]

Before reason can get started certain things must be presupposed. However, unlike modern presuppositionalists, Pascal held that these first principles could be known with certainty through the intuition of the heart. The Cartesian attempt to prove everything by reason alone was totally futile from Pascal's perspective. First principles are self-evident truths recognized intuitively by the heart. They cannot be proven by reason; they must be assumed in order for a person to even begin to reason.

Pascal was a man before his time. He saw where Descartes' rationalism would lead man. When pure rationalism (which characterized much of modern philosophy) failed to produce the answers expected of it, it eventually collapsed into skepticism and irrationalism (post-modernism). This was due to the failure to recognize the limits of reason.

The time is now ripe for Pascalian apologetics. When pure rationalism is scorned, Christian apologists must learn to speak to the hearts, as well as the minds, of men. And we can learn this art if we sit at the feet of Blaise Pascal.

THE PARADOX OF MAN

Pascal believed that only the Christian religion rightly explained man's nature. Man is both wretched and great. Many religions recognize man's greatness, but fail to see man's wretchedness. The New Age movement is an example; man is God and sin is an illusion. Other religions accept man's wretchedness but ignore his greatness. Secular Humanists consider man to be an animal; Behaviorists view man as a machine. Only Christianity sees man for what he really is; man is both wretched and great.

Pascal concludes that the Christian doctrines of creation and the fall alone adequately explain the paradox of man. Pascal believed that man's greatness could be explained in the fact that man was created in God's image. And he argues that man would not understand his wretchedness unless he had some remembrance of a former greatness from which he had fallen. Pascal wrote:

> Man is only a reed, the weakest in nature, but he is a thinking reed. There is no need for the whole universe to take up arms to crush him: a vapour, a drop of water is enough to kill him. But even if the universe were to crush him, man would still be nobler than his slayer, because he knows that he is dying and the advantage the universe has over him. The universe knows none of this. Thus all our dignity consists in thought. (200)

> Man's greatness comes from knowing he is wretched: a tree does not know it is wretched. Thus it is wretched to know one is wretched, but there is a greatness in knowing one is wretched. (114)

> All these examples of wretchedness prove his greatness. It is the wretchedness of a great lord,

the wretchedness of a dispossessed king. (116)

Man's greatness and wretchedness are so evident that the true religion must necessarily teach us that there is in man some great principle of greatness and some great principle of wretchedness. (149)

Man is neither angel nor beast. . . (678)

There are in faith two equally constant truths. One is that man in the state of his creation, or in the state of grace, is exalted above the whole of nature, made like unto God and sharing in His divinity. The other is that in the state of corruption and sin he has fallen from that first state and has become like the beasts. . . (131)

For a religion to be true it must have known our nature; it must have known its greatness and smallness, and the reason for both. What other religion but Christianity has known this? (215)

The dilemma of man, that he is both great and wretched, is easy to document. The gap between animals and man is too great for evolution to adequately explain. No animal species will ever produce a Plato or Aristotle. Yet, the cruelty of man waged against man is unheard of in the animal kingdom. No animal species will ever produce a Hitler or Stalin.

Only Christianity with its doctrine of creation and the fall can adequately explain both aspects of man. Twentieth-century Christian apologists such as Francis Schaeffer[11] and Ravi Zacharias[12] continued the Pascalian tradition by using man's greatness and wretchedness as evidence for Christianity.

THE HUMAN CONDITION

Pascal sees the human condition as ultimately a one-way road to death. Death is a fact from which all men try to hide; nonetheless, it is a fact. We will all eventually die. . . and we know it. However, we live as if we will never die. The words of Pascal are haunting:

> Imagine a number of men in chains, all under sentence of death, some of whom are each day butchered in the sight of the others; those remaining see their own condition in that of their fellows, and looking at each other with grief and despair await their turn. This is an image of the human condition. (434)

> It is absurd of us to rely on the company of our fellows, as wretched and helpless as we are; they will not help us; we shall die alone. (151)

> The last act is bloody, however fine the rest of the play. They throw earth over your head and it is finished forever. (165)

> Let us ponder these things, and then say whether it is not beyond doubt that the only good thing in this life is the hope of another life. . . (427)

> We desire truth and find in ourselves nothing but uncertainty. We seek happiness and find only wretchedness and death. (401)

> God alone is man's true good. . . (148)

All men will die, and they know they will die. Yet, they do not all live lives of despair. Pascal explains how man copes despite his hopeless condition.

MAN'S RESPONSE TO HIS HOPELESS CONDITION

Pascal states that man responds to his hopeless condition in three ways: diversion, indifference, and self-deception. Rather than admit human wretchedness and death and look for a cure, we would rather ignore the human condition and lie to ourselves. Pascal wrote concerning diversion:

> Diversion. Being unable to cure death, wretchedness and ignorance, men have decided, in order to be happy, not to think about such things. (133)

> If our condition were truly happy we should not need to divert ourselves from thinking about it. (70)

> We run heedlessly into the abyss after putting something in front of us to stop us seeing it. (166)

> I can quite see that it makes a man happy to be diverted from contemplating his private miseries by making him care about nothing else but dancing well. . . (137)

Contemporary society has multitudes of diversions. Television, radio, computers, the theater, sports events, and our careers are just a few of the many ways we can occupy ourselves so as to keep our focus off of our wretchedness and inevitable death. If the NFL went on strike this football season, would church attendance increase? We need to remind our fellow man that eternal matters are of more importance than the temporary pleasures of this life.

Recently, I saw a truck with a bumper sticker which read, "Everyone needs something to believe in. . . I believe

I'll have another beer." Pascal was right; man diverts his attention through temporary pleasures to hide the truths he wishes to ignore.

Indifference is another way in which man avoids dealing with his coming death:

> The immortality of the soul is something of such vital importance to us, affecting us so deeply, that one must have lost all feeling not to care about knowing the facts of the matter. . . Thus the fact that there exist men who are indifferent to the loss of their being and the peril of an eternity of wretchedness is against nature. With everything else they are quite different; they fear the most trifling things, foresee and feel them; and the same man who spends so many days and nights in fury and despair at losing some office or at some imaginary affront to his honour is the very one who knows that he is going to lose everything through death but feels neither anxiety nor emotion. It is a monstrous thing to see one and the same heart at once so sensitive to minor things and so strangely insensitive to the greatest. (427)

The roar of a crowd at the Super Bowl is deafening, but place that same crowd into a church, and there will be only silence. They are passionate about the outcome of a football game, but indifferent concerning the eternal things of God.

The unsaved man not only ignores the horror of his wretchedness and impending death through diversion and indifference. He also chooses to deceive himself and others in an attempt to hide from the truth:

Self-love. The nature of self-love and of this human self is to love only self and consider only self. . . it takes every care to hide its faults both from itself and others, and cannot bear to have them pointed out or noticed. . . For is it not true that we hate the truth and those who tell it to us, and we like them to be deceived to our advantage, and want to be esteemed by them as other than we actually are? . . . people are more wary of offending those whose friendship is most useful and enmity most dangerous. A prince can be the laughingstock of Europe and the only one to know nothing about it. (978)

Blaise Pascal saw that the use of reason alone would lead few, if any, to Christ. Pascal realized man is ruled more by his passions than by his reason. Therefore, his apologetic methodology focused on shaking men out of their indifference and removing their diversions. His apologetic reminds men that eternal issues are of far greater worth than mere temporary ones. Pascal did not try to reason men into the kingdom; he attempted to sway men to desire Christianity to be true. He encouraged men to earnestly seek the God of the Bible. Modern society is based more on pleasures and desire than on reason. Therefore, Pascal's method of defending the faith has great potential in our day.

Abstract argumentation is not appealing to most people. Pascal recognized that man would rather discuss the concrete things of everyday life. Therefore, Pascal started his apologetic where most people would feel comfortable—with the person himself. Then Pascal would attempt to take the person out of their comfort zone by revealing the hidden, unattractive truths (such as wretchedness, death, and self-deception) about the person. All this was done to reveal to the person the shallowness of this life and the need for the eternal things of God.

HISTORICAL EVIDENCES FOR THE CHRISTIAN FAITH

Pascal is not a traditional apologist, for he rejects the traditional arguments for God's existence. But, he is also not a fideist or a presuppositionalist, for no fideist or true presuppositionalist would provide historical evidences for the Christian faith:

> Prophecies. If a single man had written a book foretelling the time and manner of Jesus' coming and Jesus had come in conformity with these prophecies, this would carry infinite weight. But there is much more here. There is a succession of men over a period of 4,000 years, coming consistently and invariably one after the other, to foretell the same coming; there is an entire people proclaiming it, existing for 4,000 years to testify in a body to the certainty they feel about it, from which they cannot be deflected by whatever threats and persecutions they may suffer. This is of a quite different order of importance. (332)

> Advantages of the Jewish people. . . This people is not only of remarkable antiquity but has also lasted for a singularly long time, extending continuously from its origin to the present day. For whereas the peoples of Greece and Italy, of Sparta, Athens, Rome, and others who came so much later have perished so long ago, these still exist, despite the efforts of so many powerful kings who have tried a hundred times to wipe them out. . . They have always been preserved however, and their preservation was foretold. . . (451)

. . . Thus instead of concluding that there are no true miracles because there are so many false ones, we must on the contrary say that there certainly are true miracles since there are so many false ones, and that the false ones are only there because true ones exist. (734)

Proofs of Jesus Christ. The hypothesis that the Apostles were knaves is quite absurd. Follow it out to the end and imagine these twelve men meeting after Jesus' death and conspiring to say that he had risen from the dead. This means attacking all the powers that be. The human heart is singularly susceptible to fickleness, to change, to promises, to bribery. One of them had only to deny his story under these inducements, or still more because of possible imprisonment, tortures and death, and they would all have been lost. Follow that out. (310)

The Apostles were either deceived or deceivers. Either supposition is difficult, for it is not possible to imagine that a man has risen from the dead. While Jesus was with them he could sustain them, but afterwards, if he did not appear to them, who did make them act? (322)

Pascal was willing to use historical evidences as proof for the Christian faith. He viewed the prophecies that Jesus had fulfilled and the preservation of the Jewish people despite centuries of persecution as strong evidence for Christianity. Pascal considered miracles, especially Christ's resurrection from the dead, to be valuable ammunition for the arsenal of the apologist. Pascal did not tell unbelievers to "just believe." He gave them evidence for the truth of Christianity. Still, he refused to use reason alone; his apologetic attempted to reach the whole man, not just his mind.

PASCAL'S WAGER

The climax of the Pascalian apologetic is known as Pascal's wager. Pascal pleads with his readers to wager their lives on God:

> . . . let us say: 'Either God is or he is not.' But to which view shall we be inclined? Reason cannot decide this question. Infinite chaos separates us. At the far end of this infinite distance a coin is being spun which will come down heads or tails. How will you wager? Reason cannot make you choose either, reason cannot prove either wrong. . . . Yes, but you must wager. There is no choice, you are already committed. Which will you choose then? . . . Let us weigh up the gain and the loss involved in calling heads that God exists. Let us assess the two cases: if you win you win everything, if you lose you lose nothing. Do not hesitate then; wager that he does exist. . . . And thus, since you are obliged to play, you must be renouncing reason if you hoard your life rather than risk it for an infinite gain, just as likely to occur as a loss amounting to nothing. . . . Thus our argument carries infinite weight, when the stakes are finite in a game where there are even chances of winning and losing and an infinite prize to be won. (418)

Pascal tells his readers that we must wager our lives

on either God existing or God not existing. Reason, due to its limitations, cannot make the decision for us. We cannot avoid choosing sides; for, to not wager is equivalent with wagering against God.

If you wager on God, there are only two possible outcomes. If He exists, you win eternal life. If He does not exist, you lose nothing.

However, if you wager against God existing, there are also only two possible consequences. If He does not exist, you win nothing. But, if He does exist, you lose everything.

Therefore, since you have nothing to lose and everything to gain, the wise man will wager that God exists. Pascal is not trying to rationally prove God's existence with this argument. Instead, he is attempting to persuade the unbeliever that it wise to live as if God exists, while it is unwise to live as if God does not exist. Pascal believed that everyone who sincerely seeks God will find Him (Jeremiah 29:13).

The wager argument is Pascal's attempt to convince the nonbeliever to seek God. Pascal wrote:

> . . . there are only two classes of persons who can be called reasonable: those who serve God with all their heart because they know him and those who seek him with all their heart because they do not know him. (427)

Richard Creel illustrates the strength of Pascal's wager with the following words:

> It would not be irrational for me to continue to search a lake and its environs for a child that I concede, along with everyone else, has almost certainly drowned. If you ask me if I believe that the

child has drowned, then I will say "yes"—but I will add that I hope that my belief is false and that I think that my continued efforts to find the child alive are justified by the great good that would obtain were I to succeed. . . . In conclusion, when God is thought of as infinitely perfect goodness, it seems consummately rational to hope that there is a God and to live as though there is, as long as there is no conclusive proof that there is not.[13]

CONCLUSION

Blaise Pascal had a unique apologetic methodology. He was not a traditional apologist, for he denied that the traditional theistic proofs would persuade nonbelievers. He was not a fideist, for he defended the faith. And, he was not a pure presuppositionalist, for he used historical evidences to prove the truth of Christianity. At best, Pascal's methodology could be classified as a type of psychological apologetics.[14] For he attempted to speak to the entire man, not just his intellect.

Today, many people are not concerned about finding rational truth. But, ironically, they are very concerned about their existential experience. Many people seek meaning in life; they also want their deepest desires to be satisfied. At the same time, many people are reluctant to admit their faults.

Therefore, the Pascalian apologetic methodology has great potential for contemporary society, for Pascal forces us to look at ourselves in the mirror. He forces us to see ourselves as we are: wretched, miserable people who will all eventually die. Pascal then tugs at our hearts and declares to us that only in Jesus can life have meaning. Only in Jesus can we find satisfaction and forgiveness. Only in Jesus can death, our greatest enemy, be defeated.

Pascal beseeches contemporary man to wager on the

God of the Bible. He calls us to seek God with all our being, for Pascal knows that if we seek Him with all our being, we will find Him. And if we find Him, we win eternity.

ENDNOTES

[1] *The World Book Encyclopedia* (Chicago: World Book, Inc., 1985), vol. 15, "Blaise Pascal," by Phillip S. Jones, 167.

[2] Thomas V. Morris, *Making Sense of It All* (Grand Rapids: William B. Eerdmans Publishing Company, 1992), 8.

[3] Ibid., 10.

[4] Ibid., entire book.

[5] Peter Kreeft, *Christianity for Modern Pagans* (San Francisco: Ignatius Press, 1993), entire book.

[6] Blaise Pascal, *Pensees,* trans. A. J. Krailsheimer, (London: Penguin Books, 1966). (Number of Pensee listed in parenthesis after quote.)

[7] Kreeft, 228. See also Frederick Copleston, *A History of Philosophy* vol. IV (New York: Image Books, 1960), 166-167.

[8] Kreeft, 228.

[9] Morris, 183.

[10] Kreeft, 235.

[11] Francis A. Schaeffer, *Trilogy* (Wheaton: Crossway Books, 1990), 109-114.

[12] Ravi Zacharias, *Can Man Live Without God?* (Dallas: Word Publishing, 1994), 133-145.

[13] Richard E. Creel, "Agatheism: A Justification of the Rationality of Devotion to God," *Faith and Philosophy,* vol. 10 (January 1993): 40, 45.

[14] Gordon R. Lewis, *Testing Christianity's Truth Claims* (Lanham: University Press of America, 1990), 231-253.

THE CREED OF 1 CORINTHIANS 15:3-8:

ANCIENT EVIDENCE FOR CHRIST'S RESURRECTION

It is often assumed by anti-Christian skeptics that the resurrection of Jesus Christ from the dead is nothing more than an ancient myth or legend, having no basis in historical fact. However, this is not the case. In the Apostle Paul's First Letter to the Corinthians, we find excellent eyewitness testimony concerning the resurrection that nearly dates back to the event itself. The Apostle Paul wrote:

> For I delivered to you as of first importance what I also received, that Christ died for our sins according to the Scriptures, and that He was buried, and that He was raised on the third day according to the Scriptures, and that He appeared to Cephas, then to the twelve. After that He appeared to more than

five hundred brethren at one time, most of whom remain until now, but some have fallen asleep; then He appeared to James, then to all the apostles; and last of all, as it were to one untimely born, He appeared to me also (1 Corinthians 15:3-8).

Most New Testament scholars, liberal and conservative alike, agree that this passage is an ancient creed or hymn formulated by the early church. In this paper, I will briefly discuss the results of the scholarly research done concerning this passage. I will attempt to ascertain the approximate date of Paul's First Letter to the Corinthians, as well as the approximate date of the origination of this ancient creed. The content of this creed will be examined, and the evidential value of this creed will be noted.

THE DATE OF 1 CORINTHIANS

In our task of ascertaining when the creed of 1 Corinthians 15 was created, it is first necessary to determine when Paul wrote 1 Corinthians. In this way, we will establish the latest possible date for the creed. We can then work our way back in time from that date, following any clues based upon the internal evidence found in the creed itself.

Christian philosopher J. P. Moreland has correctly stated that for the past one hundred years almost all New Testament critics have accepted the Pauline authorship of 1 Corinthians.[1] A comparison of 1 Corinthians 16 with Acts 18, 19, and 20 provides strong evidence that 1 Corinthians was written by Paul in 55AD while in Ephesus.[2] Scholars such as John A. T. Robinson, Henry C. Thiessen, A. T. Robertson, Douglas Moo, Leon Morris, and D. A. Carson all concur that 1 Corinthians was written in the mid 50's AD.[3]

THE DATE OF THE CREED

We have established 55AD as the date for the composition of 1 Corinthians. This means that the ancient creed quoted by Paul in 1 Corinthians 15:3-8 had to originate before this date. However, there is strong evidence found in the creed itself that points to its development at a much earlier time.

Christian apologist Gary Habermas discusses at least eight pieces of evidence from within the creed that indicate a very early date. First, the terms "delivered" and "received" have been shown to be technical rabbinic terms used for the passing on of sacred tradition.[4] Second, Paul admitted that this statement was not his own creation and that he had received it from others.[5] Third, scholars agree that some of the words in the creed are non-Pauline terms and are clearly Jewish. These phrases include "for our sins," "according to the Scriptures," "He has been raised," "the third day," "He was seen," and "the twelve."[6] Fourth, the creed is organized into a stylized and parallel form; it appears to have been an oral creed or hymn in the early church.[7] Fifth, the creed shows evidence of being of a Semitic origin and, thus, points to a source that predates Paul's translation of it into Greek.[8] This can be seen in the use of "Cephas" for Peter, for "Cephas" is Aramaic for Peter (which is Petros in the Greek).[9] Moreland notes additional evidence for the Semitic origin of this creed by relating that the poetic style of the creed is clearly Hebraic.[10] Sixth, Habermas reasons that Paul probably received this creed around 36-38AD, just three years after his conversion, when he met with Peter and James in Jerusalem (as recorded by Paul in Galatians 1:18-19).[11] Jesus' death occurred around 30AD, and Paul was converted between 33 and 35AD.[12] Seventh, Habermas states that, due to the above information, "numerous critical theologians" date the creed "from three to eight years after Jesus' crucifixion."[13]

Eighth, since it would have taken a period of time for the beliefs to become formalized into a creed or hymn, the beliefs behind the creed must date back to the event itself.[14]

THE CONTENT OF THE CREED

We have provided strong evidence that the creed of 1 Corinthians 15:3-8 originated between three to eight years after Christ's crucifixion, and that the beliefs which underlie this creed must therefore go back to the event itself. Now we must briefly examine the content of this ancient creed.

First, the creed, as stated in this passage, mentions the death and burial of Christ. Second, it states that Christ was raised on the third day. Third, it lists several post-resurrection appearances of Christ. These include appearances to Peter, to the twelve apostles, to over 500 persons at one time, to James (the Lord's brother), to all the apostles, and, finally an appearance to Paul himself.

It should be noted that scholars differ as to the exact contents of this ancient creed in its most primitive form. Due to the brevity of this paper, I will merely express my own opinion on the matter. I believe that Paul added verse eight (detailing his own eyewitness account) to the original creed, as well as a portion of verse six (a reminder that most of the 500 witnesses were still alive). This in no way lessons the force of this ancient creed. In fact, it strengthens it as evidence for the resurrection, for Paul adds his own testimony and encourages his readers to question the many eyewitnesses still living in his day. Even scholars who disagree with my view still accept a large enough portion of the creed for it to be considered a valuable piece of eyewitness evidence for the resurrection of Christ from the dead.

THE EVIDENTIAL VALUE OF THE CREED

Having argued for a very early date for its origin, we must now ascertain the evidential value of this creed. Simply stated, the early date of the 1 Corinthians 15 creed proves that the resurrection accounts found in the New Testament are not legends. Christian philosopher William Lane Craig, while commenting on the work of the great

Roman historian A. N. Sherwin-White, stated that "even two generations is too short a time span to allow legendary tendencies to wipe out the hard core of historical facts."[15] If two generations is not enough time for legends to develop, then there is no way that a resurrection legend could emerge in only three to eight years.

It should also be noted that, in this creed, Paul is placing his apostolic credentials on the line by encouraging his Corinthian critics to check out his account with the eyewitnesses who were still alive. These eyewitnesses not only included over 500 people, but also Peter, James, and the other apostles—the recognized leaders of the early church (Galatians 2:9). It is highly improbable that Paul would fabricate the creed and jeopardize his own position in the early church.

Finally, it should be obvious to any open-minded person who examines the evidence that Paul was a man of integrity. He was not lying. Not only did he put his reputation and position in the early church on the line, but he was also willing to suffer and die for Christ. Men do not die for what they know to be a hoax. Paul was a reliable and sincere witness to the resurrection of Christ.

CONCLUSION

The creed of 1 Corinthians 15:3-8 provides us with reliable eyewitness testimony for the bodily resurrection of Jesus Christ. Not only did Paul testify that he had seen the risen Christ, but he also identified many other witnesses to the resurrection that could have been interrogated. Contrary to the futile speculations of liberal scholars, Paul was not devising myths behind closed doors. No, from the beginning he was preaching a risen Savior who had conquered death and the grave, a risen Savior who had met him on the road to Damascus and changed his life forever.

ENDNOTES

[1] J. P. Moreland, *Scaling the Secular City* (Grand Rapids: Baker Book House, 1987), 148.

[2] Leon Morris, *1 Corinthians* (Leicester, England: Inter-Varsity Press, 1995), 30-31.

[3] John A. T. Robinson, *Redating the New Testament* (SCM Press, 1976), 54. Henry C. Thiessen, *Introduction to the New Testament* (Grand Rapids: William B. Eerdmans Publishing Company, 1987), 205. A. T. Robertson, *Word Pictures in the New Testament,* vol. 4, (Grand Rapids: Baker Book House, 1931), xvi. D. A. Carson, Douglas J. Moo, and Leon Morris, *An Introduction to the New Testament* (Grand Rapids: Zondervan Publishing House, 1992), 283.

[4] Gary R. Habermas, *Ancient Evidence for the Life of Jesus* (Nashville: Thomas Nelson Publishers, 1984), 124.

[5] Ibid.

[6] Ibid.

[7] Ibid., 125.

[8] Ibid.

[9] Ibid.

[10] Moreland, 150.

[11] Habermas, 125.

[12] Ibid.

[13] Ibid.

[14] Ibid.

[15] William Lane Craig, *Reasonable Faith* (Wheaton: CrossWay Books, 1994), 285.

ABOUT THE AUTHOR

Phil Fernandes is the senior pastor of Trinity Bible Fellowship and the founder and president of the Institute of Biblical Defense, an apologetics ministry which trains Christians in the defense of the faith. Both ministries are located in Bremerton, Washington.

Dr. Fernandes has earned a Ph.D. in philosophy of religion from Greenwich University, a Master of Arts in Religion from Liberty University, and a Bachelor of Theology from Columbia Evangelical Seminary.

He has lectured and debated in defense of Christianity on college campuses and in public schools. Dr. Fernandes has debated Dr. Michael Martin (one of America's leading atheists, Professor of Philosophy at Boston University), Dr. Peter John (Professor of Philosophy at Lower Columbia College), Jeff Lowder (President of Atheist Infidels), and Rev. Farley Maxwell (President of Parents and Friends of Lesbians and Gays).

Dr. Fernandes currently teaches philosophy and apologetics for Columbia Evangelical Seminary and Cascade Bible College. He is a member of the following professional societies: the Evangelical Theological Society, the Evangelical Philosophical Society, and the Society of Christian Philosophers.

Dr. Fernandes is the author of three books: *The Decay of a Nation: The Need for National Revival* (1987), *The God Who Sits Enthroned: Evidence for God's Existence* (1997), and *No Other Gods: A Defense of Biblical Christianity* (1998). Dr. Fernandes also writes a monthly religious column for *The Bremerton Sun*.

Dr. Fernandes resides in Bremerton, Washington with his lovely wife Cathy. They have a grown daughter, Melissa, who is married to Tim Smith. In 1997, Tim and Melissa became the proud parents of Nathan Michael Smith.

Books by Dr. Fernandes and more than 400 audio cassette lectures given by Dr. Fernandes can be purchased from the Institute of Biblical Defense through the address or phone number listed below:

The Institute of Biblical Defense
P. O. Box 3264
Bremerton, WA. 98310

(360) 698-7382
www.biblicaldefense.org

J. P. MORELAND'S
ENDORSEMENT OF
THE INSTITUTE OF BIBLICAL DEFENSE

"It comes as no surprise to the reflective Christian that there is a great need for believers who are able to defend the faith intelligently. For that ability to be developed one first must have the right intellectual tools for the job. This is where IBD can help. The programs offered through IBD provide the student with a good foundation in apologetics and introduces him or her to the labor of reason. I recommend IBD for anyone wanting to gain fundamental skills for defending the faith or as a good first step for those wanting to pursue advanced studies in philosophy and theology."

Dr. J. P. Moreland
Professor of Apologetics
Talbot School of Theology, Biola University

Printed in the United States
82426LV00002B/193-207